SNOWFLAKES AT MIDNIGHT

copyright 2019 by Shalina Markin

All snowflake designs were originally drawn on
SnowDays.me by Shalina Markin

Other books by Shalina Markin:

Poems on the Naughty List (2018)
Of Muses and Mischief (2018)
Frost at Twilight (2019)

SNOWFLAKES

AT

MIDNIGHT

By

Shalina Markin

DEDICATION

To my friends and fellow flakers on SnowDays.
You are awesome and thank you for your
support and kindness over the years.

A special thanks to X, because you have been
an inspiration to many, and a friend I am
thankful to have met on SnowDays. We made
flake babies. XD

My family- thank you all for your love and
believing in me.

To SnowDays.me I thank you for many years of
fun.

The Snow Queen; thank you for creating a
virtual world to be a magical place and a
garden for our flakes to live forever.

To Sam and Sophia- you encourage me with
your gentle wisdom, love, and humor.

INTRODUCTION

One of my fondest memories from childhood was cutting snowflakes. Trying to make the perfect flake with dull child-friendly scissors was hard. And try to fold the paper to get a six sided snowflake was not happening. I had many round snowflakes with holes in them. And of course the floor, table and every crevasse ended up with tiny pieces of paper.

As an adult, I found myself cutting flakes once more, because they were so much fun to create. I even learned how to fold the paper properly. I kept many flakes in a box and decorated during the holidays with them. Most have since fallen apart.

And then I found a website that fed my addiction. SnowDays was a magical place. One could cut a flake with its basic program to create a virtual snowflake. I was hooked and there was no mess to clean up.

Several years have passed since my first flake in 2005 on the website, and I still find myself in awe of real snowflakes, or snow crystals as they are known in the scientific community. They are one of natures mysteries and so very beautiful, even though each one is imperfect and asymmetrical.

The flakes in this book are a small sampling of what I have made online. I darkened the background for a midnight feel. I have included my winter and Christmas themed poems for you to enjoy; which correspond with each flake.

TABLE OF CONTENTS

Sweetest snowflakes   1
Birds in Snow   2
Birth of a Storm   3
Lamppost   4
Candle in the snow   5
Old Sled   6
Carving Flakes   7
Snow Angel   8
Light Shuffles   9
Dance at Midnight   10
Delicate   11
Evaporate   12
Flakers   13
Blizzard   14
Scissor police   15
Flutter   16
Flawed Perfection   17
Gift of Snow   18
Hot Chocolate   19
Apex   20
Ice Wedging   21
Just one more   22
Khione   23
Freefalling   24
Last Light   25
Love's Thaw   26
Ornament   27
Avalanche   28

Snow Cone	29
Paper Lanterns	30
River Freeze	31
Cut and Erase	32
Shattered Glass	33
Shy angel	34
Silent Storms	35
Skate	36
Lighthouse	37
Sleigh	38
Icicles	39
Snow Prayer	40
Snowdrop petals	41
My Flakes	42
Glowing Moon	43
Frost	44
Coffee	45
Berries of Gold	46
Ugly flake	47
Winter's Song	48
Tree Topper	49
Snowgarden of the Queen	50
Reindeer	51
Bells	52
Ice Castle	53
Winter Solstice	54
Iceberg	55
Balls of Snow	56
Silence	57
Thaw my heart	58
Snow Woman	59

Littlest snowflake 60
That Scarf 61
Snow House 62
Candy twists 63
Lake in winter 64
Elven art 65
Northern Lights 66
holiday cookies 67
Ivy and Holly 68
Windowpane 69
Kris Kringle 70
Wreath 71
Noel 72
Old Man Winter 73
Pinecones 74
Carolers 75
Stained Glass 76
First Snow 77
New Year 78
Mele Kalikimaka 79
Festival of Lights 80
Gingerbread House 81
Blowing Snow 82
Flakes at Midnight 83
Hibernate 84
Fruitcake 85
Perfect trees 86

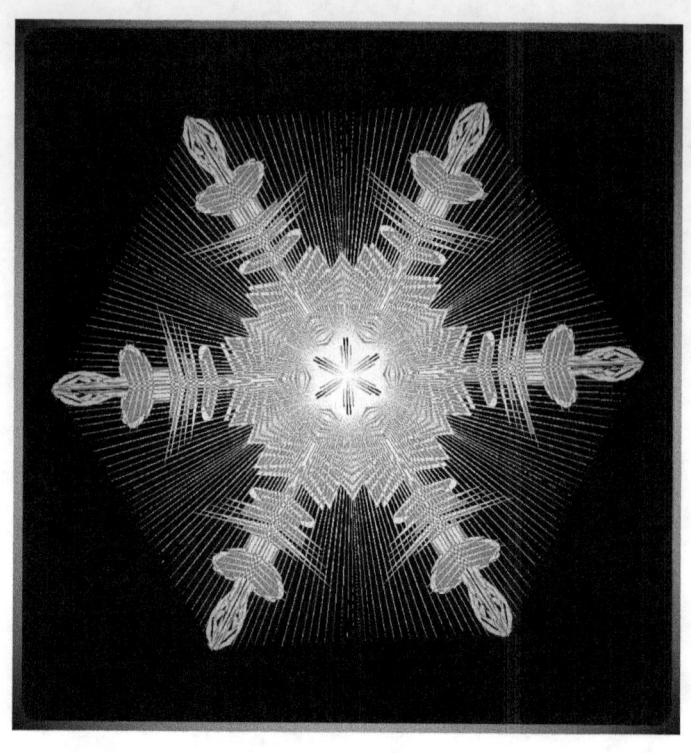

Sweetest snowflakes

If flakes were flavors; I could but taste
Wintergreen and sparkling buttermint twists
With cake batter flittering on Neptune's spear
Or pearls of spun caramel in chocolate cream
And blackberry tea with powdered sugar
Are the sweetest snowflakes I could ever eat

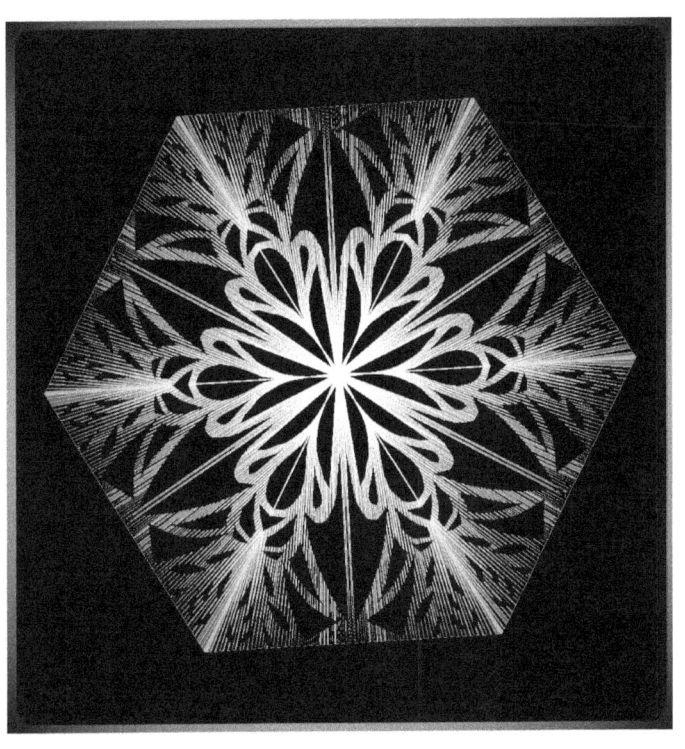

Birds in Snow

Fluttering wings of crimson in snow
With a winter coat- it's all for show
Imprinting their little claws in icy ink
To leave their mark as they flutter about
And singing cheerfully on a cold winter's day
Are birds of December that come out to play

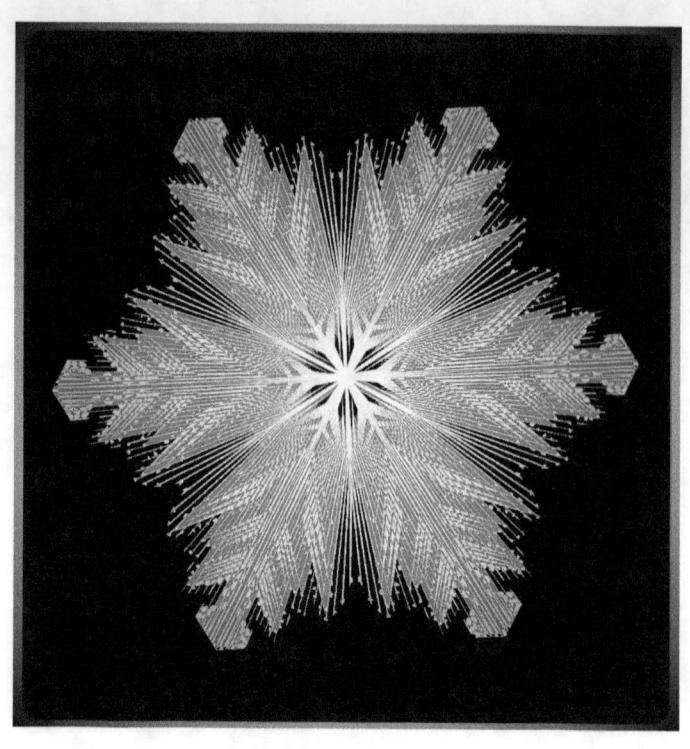

Birth of a Storm

O squall of tempest- arise and come
To fall from darkened skies- please form
And cascade vapors of crystalline clouds
Descending from heights and be born
As snowflakes twirl; tumbled and torn
A delightful display of nature- is a storm

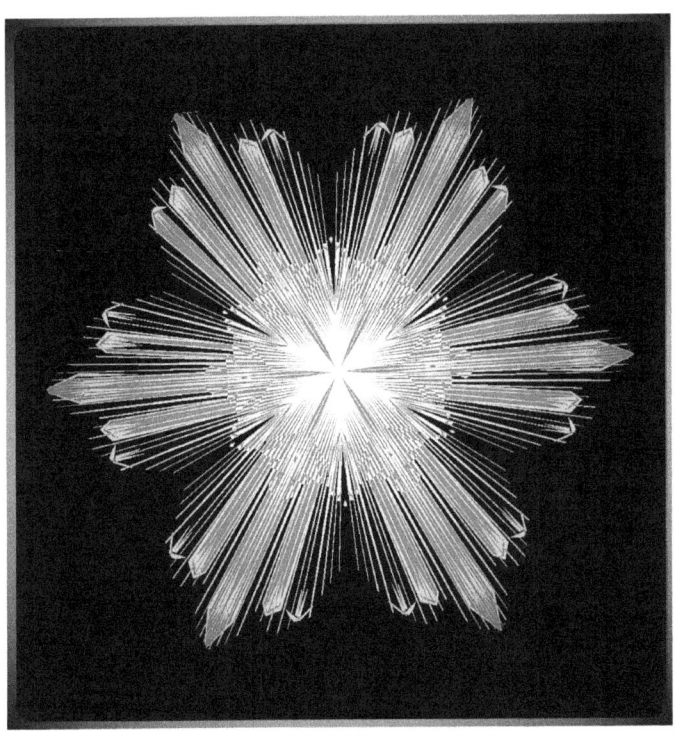

Lamppost

Guiding light casting a soft winter's glow
Of Victorian charm and a wrought iron case
With worn beveled glass and an ornate rim–
From long ago; it stands tall and bright
Making darkest evenings ever so bright,
As cascading flakes fall in arctic waves
To coil and glide throughout stormy nights

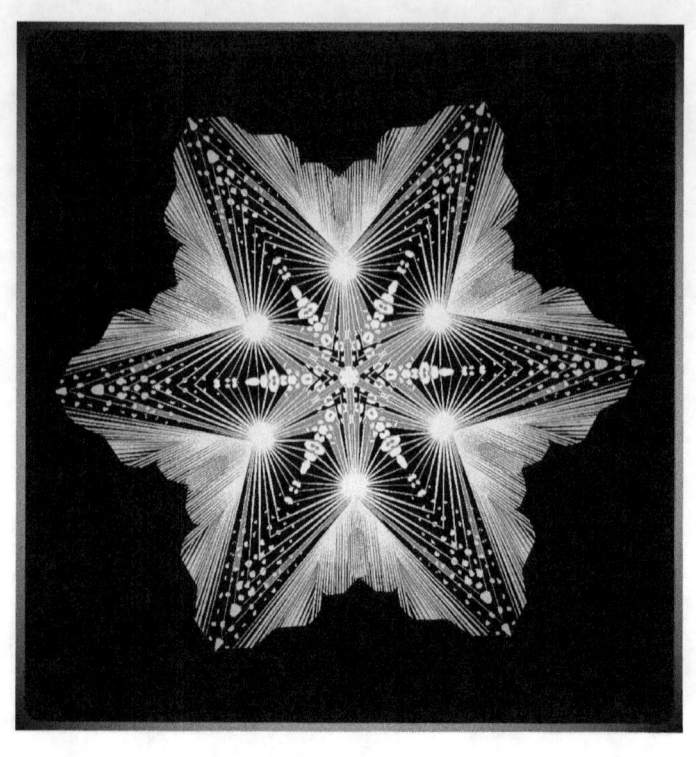

Candle in the snow

I walk carefully, and shiver in my chiffon gown
Through isolated woodlands and all alone
Towards my cottage by a stream; dark at night
But dropping my candle in new fallen snow;
Fireflies gather around and begin to glow bright
Carrying me on their wings beyond chilly night

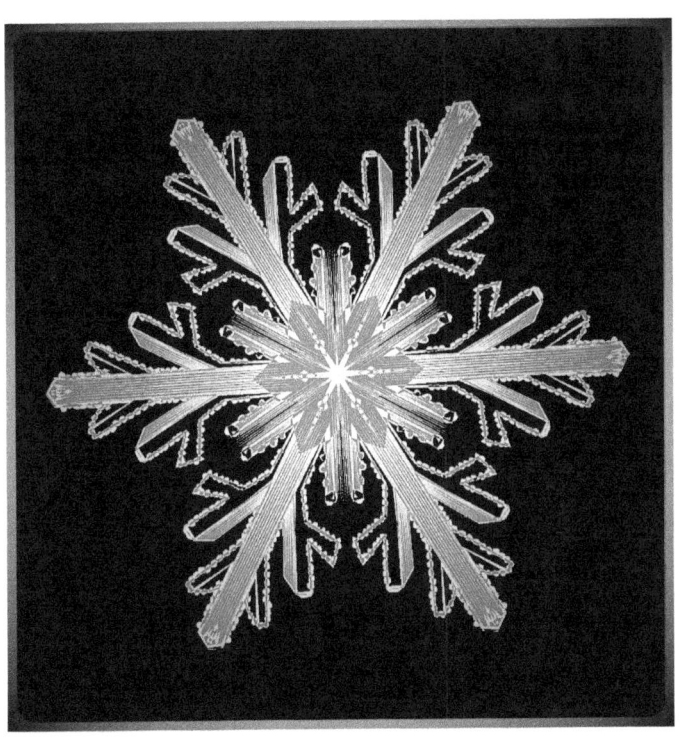

Old Sled

Steel runners and a rickety wooden board
Painted bright red and faster than a jet
Flying down slopes with a tattered rope
Guiding in and out of hills and dips
While laughing, and spinning past trees
Was that old sled; now forgotten in a shed

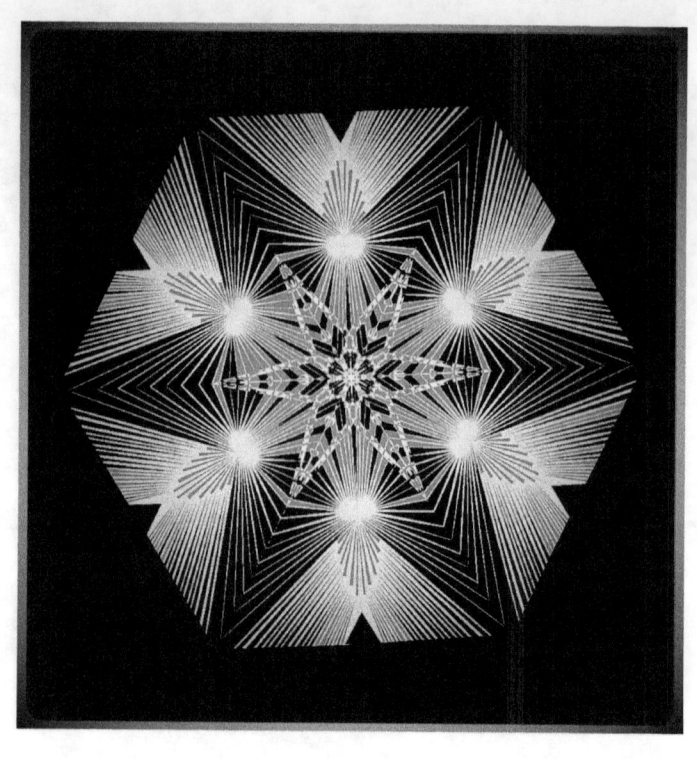

Carving Flakes

Sewn with magic and glowing silver
To carve and shave each delicate blade
With careful precision

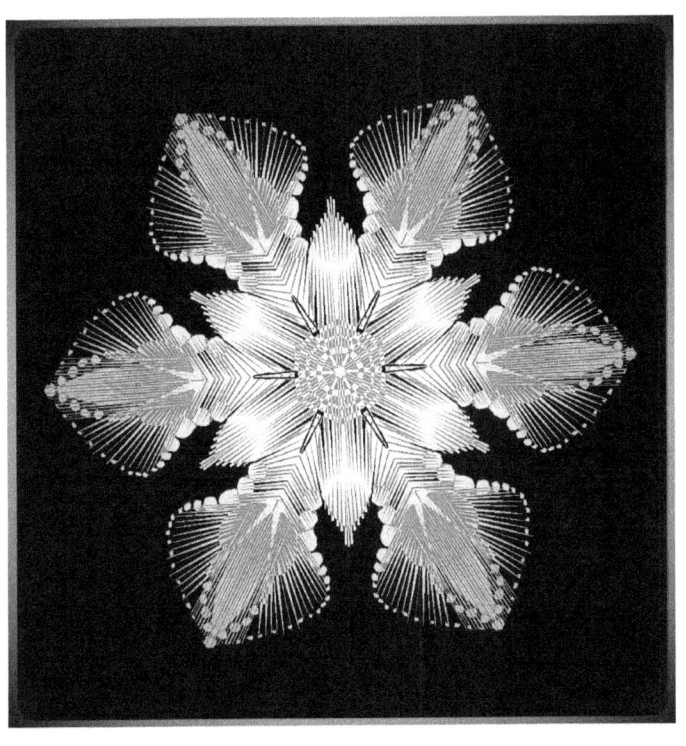

Snow Angel

Lying in a pile of white petals- so cold
And flapping arms and legs for fun
But when you stand up and look down,
Your fragile soul has left its imprint
With wings and love for all to know
That you are an angel in the snow

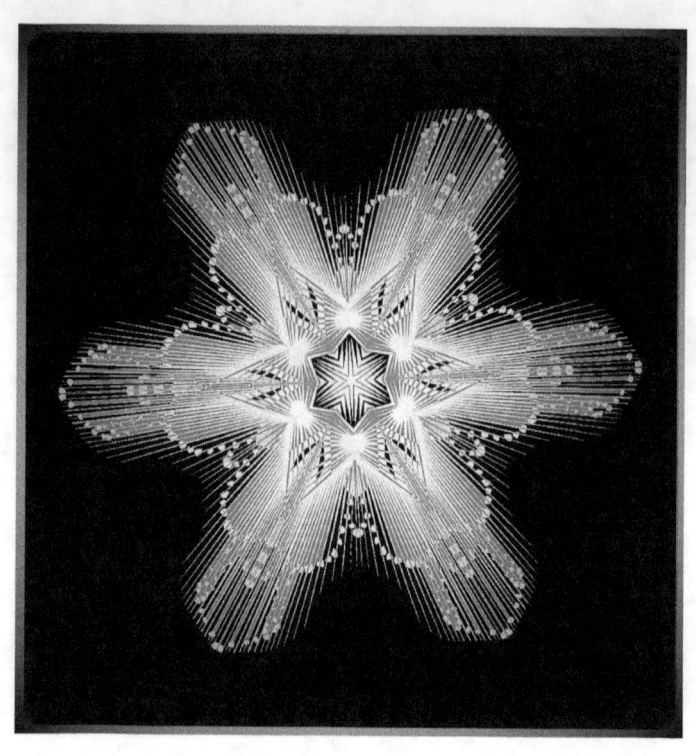

Light Shuffles

As each flake forms; silence closes in
To muffle all noise past nature's roar
Where white light shuffles in rainbows
Of sweet melodies in serendipity
To guide and fall from heaven's door

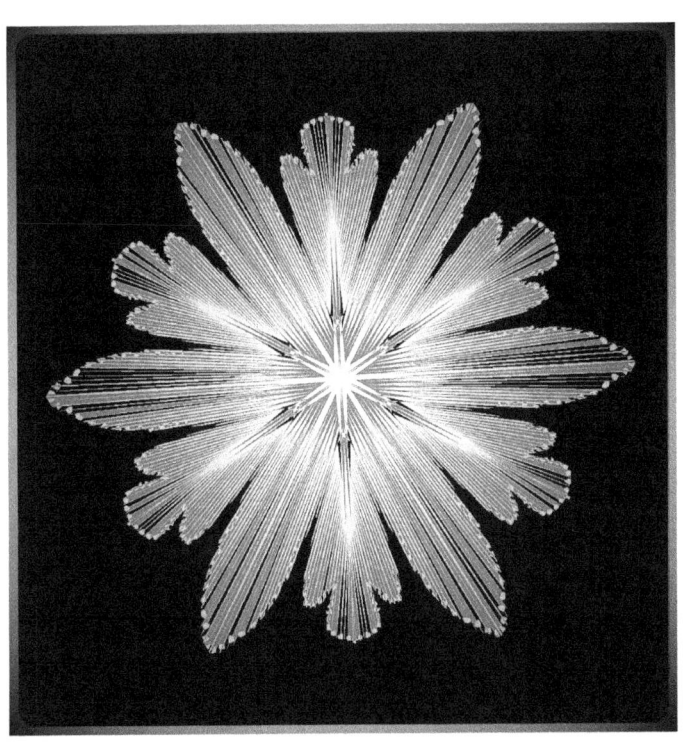

Dance at Midnight

Gossamer gowns of snowflakes and sugarplums
With turquoise glitter and blush of roses
Twirling through musical notes and frozen pens
Of calligraphy on paper and peppermint breath,
As gentle air freezes in a dance at midnight
Where glitter falls on sleek castle walls,
As sugared moonlight glows all night long

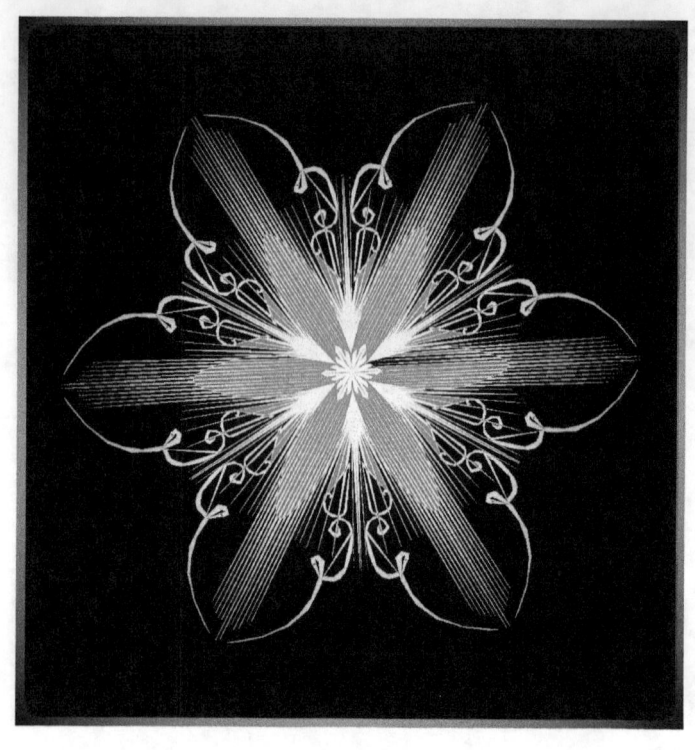

Delicate

Fall on tips of tongues and laugh–
To melt in a stinging burst of cold
And hope to find a perfect snowflake
That will land whole, and not fall apart
On mittens knitted or sweaters of wool–
To watch a gentle chef-d'oeuvre alight
And stay a while; in spite of the cold

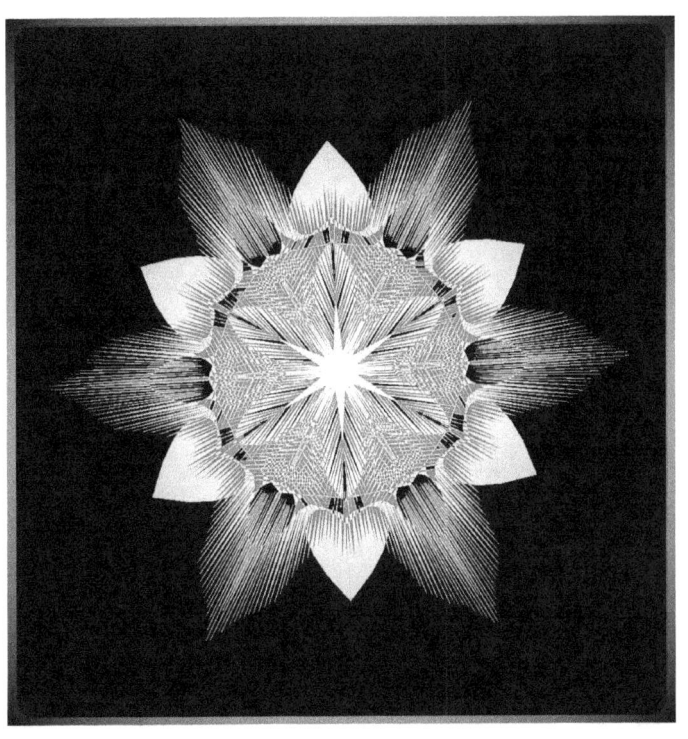

Evaporate

'Tis awe and wonder at such a sight
A fleck of water transforms midflight
With soft, yet pristine crystals spiraling;
Unaware of its loveliness; it shines bright
But careful- its cradle falls towards ground
With mist of fog and flurries surrounding it
And landing– it evaporates and falls apart

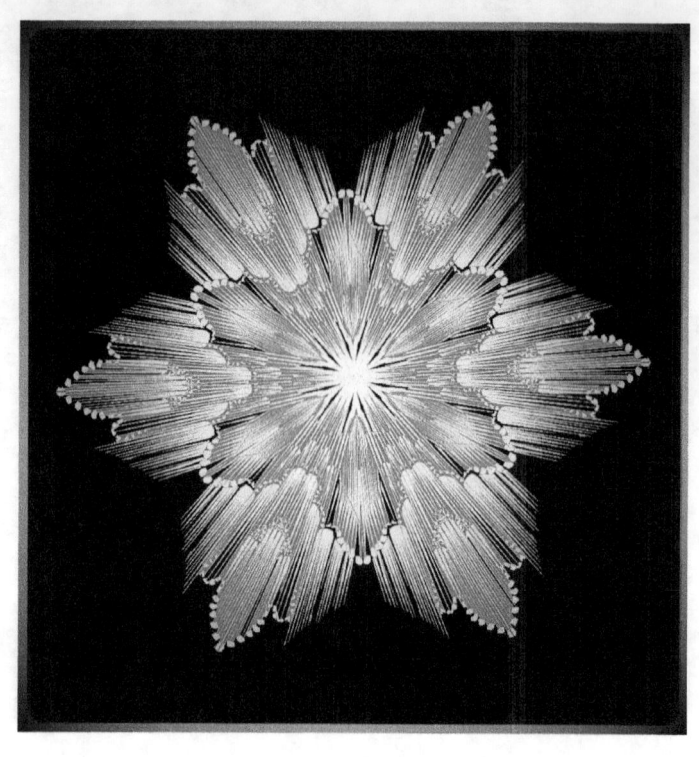

Flakers

We're a flaky lot; so I am told
Full of love and true artistic gold
Spinning yarns, as our flakes unfold
Is SnowDays; a site that never gets old

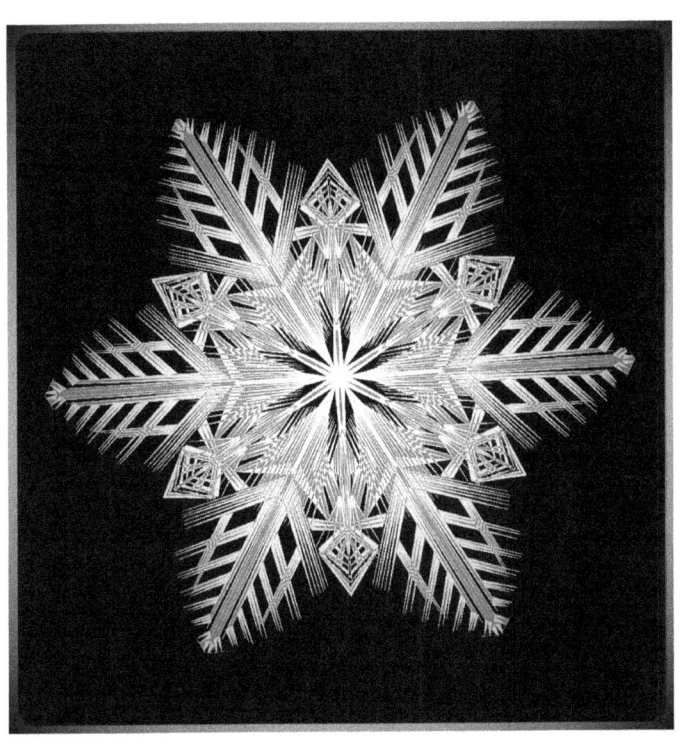

Blizzard

Clouds fizzle in drizzle of mist
And seize up with crystals in jest
As a blizzard forms in noisy fright
Only to blanket cold earth in white
And dull all color into fabulous light
Where Jack Frost glides and plays
With his ever-mischievous delight

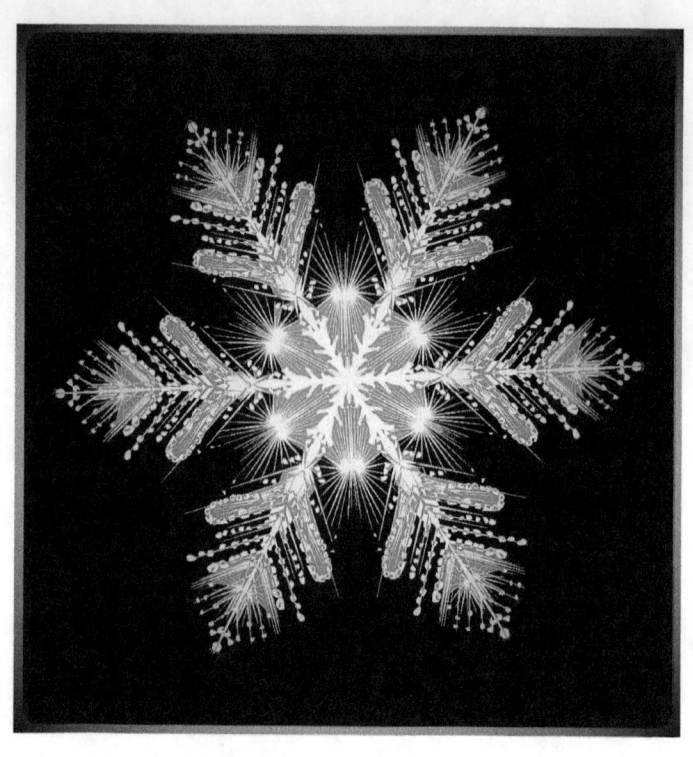

Scissor police

O, but for one more cut- they come
When a snowflake is said to be done
To halt and hinder our creative flair
As we cajole and scream with salty tears
Begging for a little longer; to no avail
As the scissor police come for us again
Because they have no mind and do not care
That our flake still looks kind of threadbare

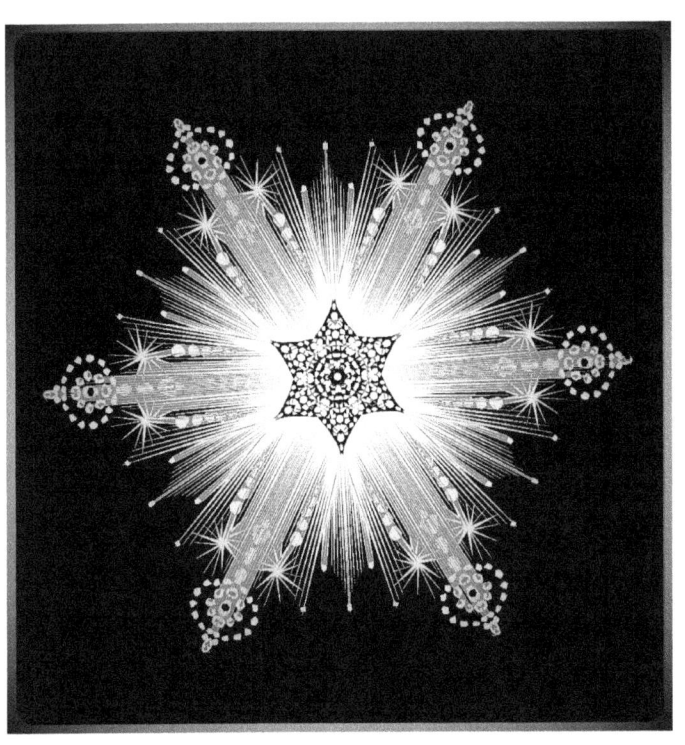

Flutter

So far away; I hear you flutter
In and out of sublime chambers
Shedding pearls and diamonds
Like a shawl of nature's wonders
That grace night skies just for me-
Are snowflakes that shine so pretty

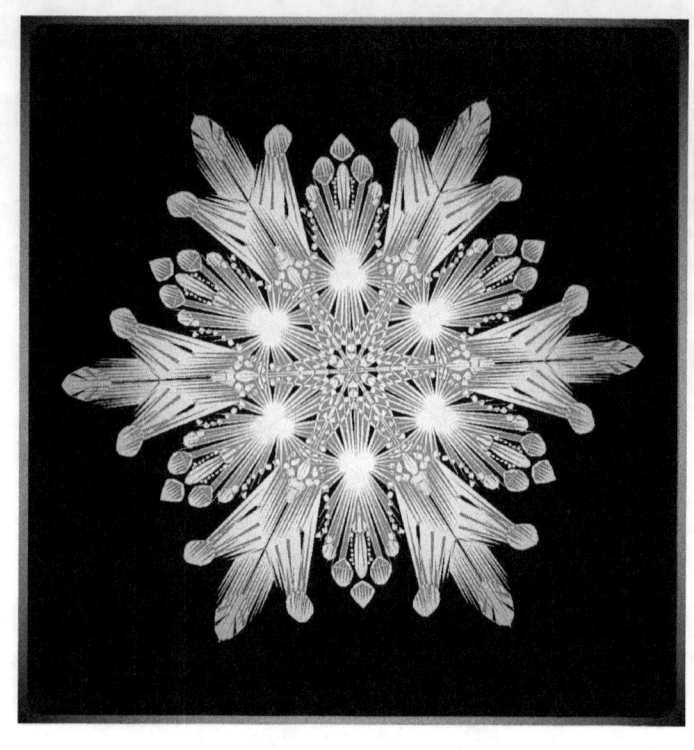

Flawed Perfection

A divine display falls from sky above
In the form of a snowflake of love
And glittery shivers in bitter cold,
But thrives in harsh conditions;
Is a crystal spread into six points
Never perfect- forever flawed
But always beautiful for all to behold

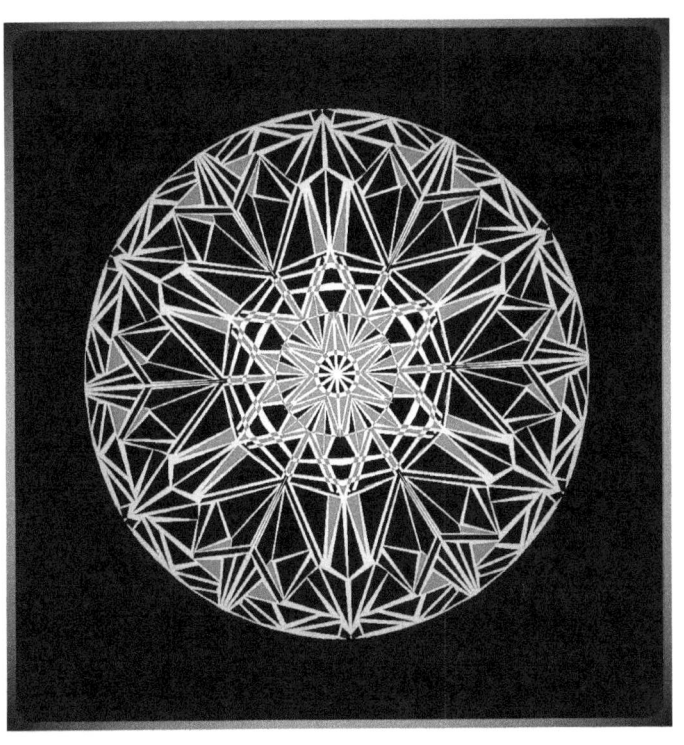

Gift of Snow

He searched far and wide; looking for a gift
To give his new bride, yet finding nothing
As years were passing by and feeling forlorn
He went towards home, and spying a snowflake
In a garden of wonder– he had his answer,
And carefully placing it on a frosted platter
That kept through a bitter November cold,
Only to find his bride was now ninety years old

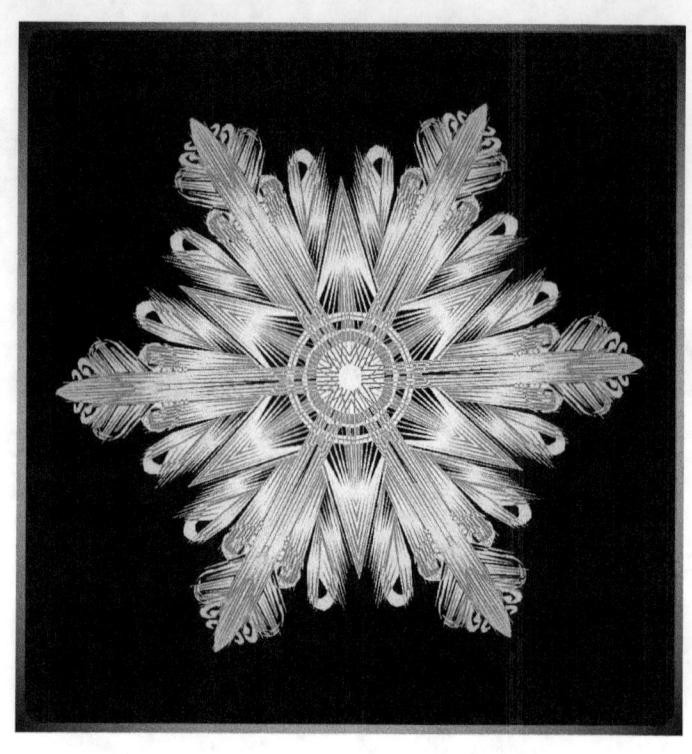

Hot Chocolate

In a candy cane mug; it steams with love
And marshmallows like snowflakes bob
In and out of hot chocolate and foam
With froth to bubble into a happy glob
On a cold winter's day- it does the job

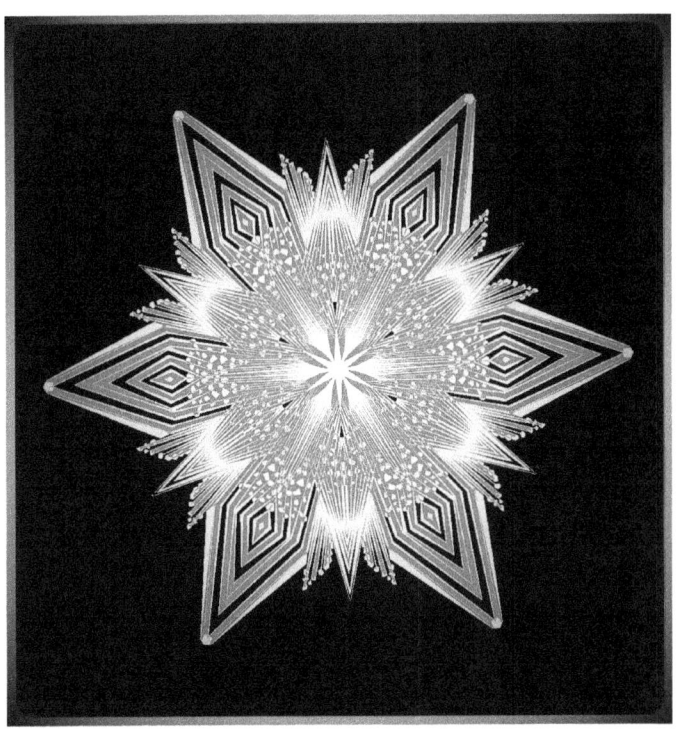

Apex

The glow of midnight sun rests gently
On wings of angels and fairy dust
To spread joy and love in every cut
Towards twilight of a million stars so bright
And paper origami fall and rise by wind
As a snowflake bends and sings with light

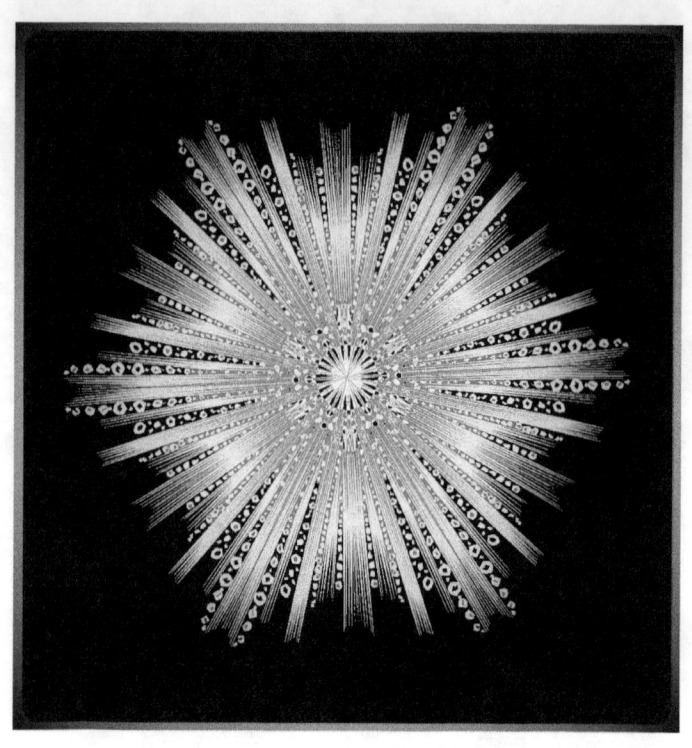

Ice Wedging

Frostbitten stones; encased in freezing snow
Icy tendrils wrap around with thinly veiled awe
Holding ever tight, until warmth of sun comes
And cracks it in half; revealing crystal geodes
With needles of glass looking like encrusted ice
In rocks that endured a cold winter's night

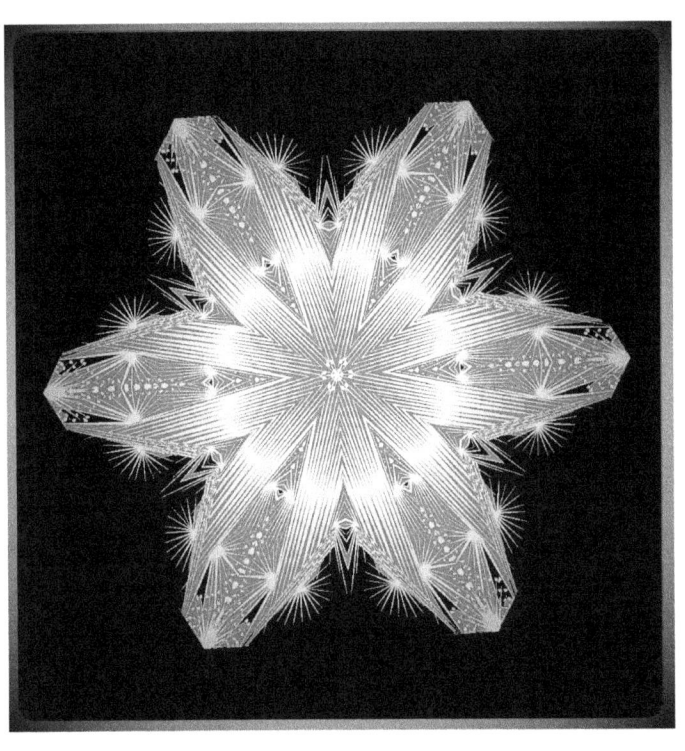

Just one more

If I could make the perfect flake
It would be the one after the next
And try as I might; I can't get it right
So, I will make just one more
And go to bed and turn out the light

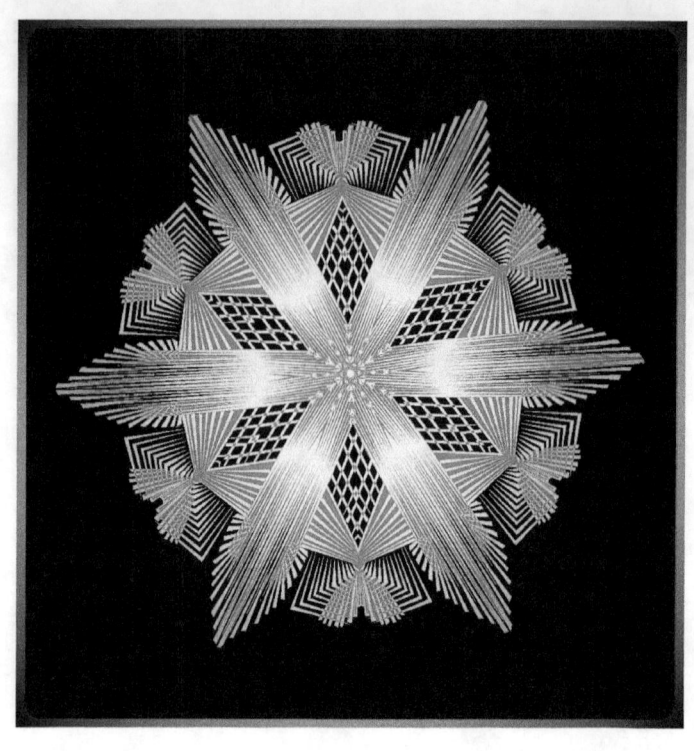

Khione

Blowing fierce wind from northern skies
She scatters snow with nymph-like wit
And flurries like cherry blossoms fall
To cover mountains and valleys below
Willing weather to obey her commands
On Mount Olympus- as goddess of snow

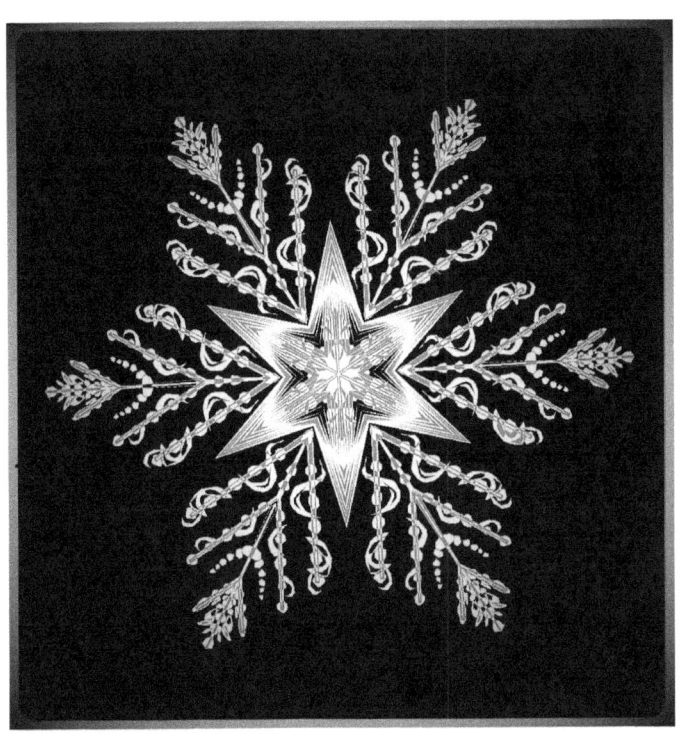

Freefalling

I'm freefalling with arms of satin
And eyelet fringe on edge of points;
Dancing in morning sky through storms
Sweeping left and right, as wind blows
My iridescent form into a pine tree
And join other flakes stuck there with me

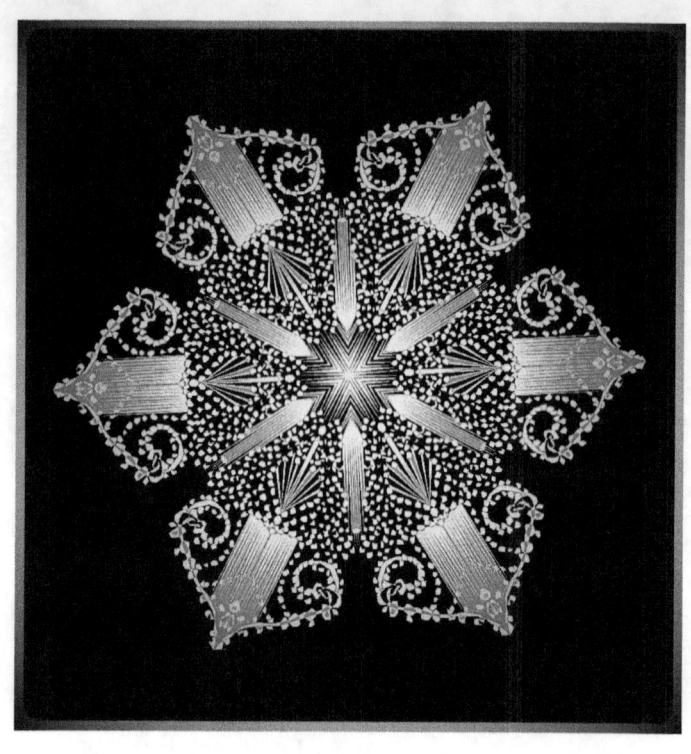

Last Light

I stay inside and watch nature unfold
As frost streaks on glass with winter's cold
Cracking in thousands of feathers to freeze
Where sun's last light reflects like amber
When wintertime temperatures drop fast
And snow falls against frozen panes in a blast
As storms build and grow, as sun sets at last

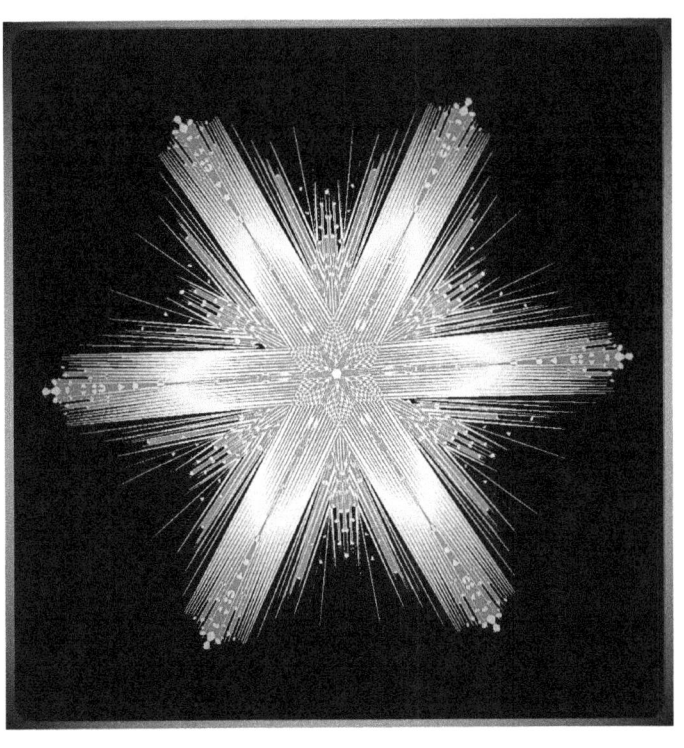

Love's Thaw

If I was a snowflake falling in love
Would you catch me?
I could melt in your arms and not care
That my icy heart becomes a drop of rain
And thaws beyond midsummer's dawn

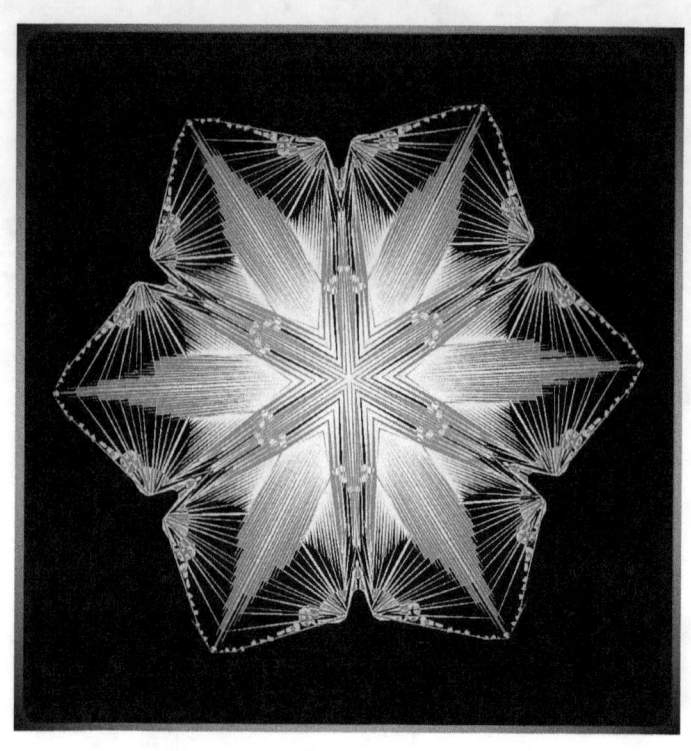

Ornament

Spun angel hair and glittery frost
Swiped across a bulb with fragile gilt
Painted with snowflakes and starlit gold
With red and green; covered in sheen
Illuminated with soft twinkling lights;
Bringing me back to my childhood of old

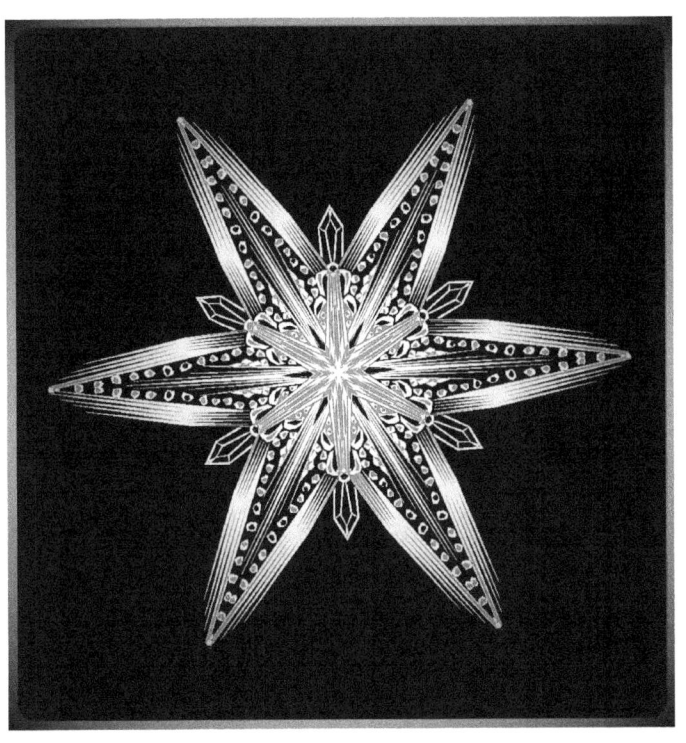

Avalanche

Trembling ice in an avalanche advances
Fusing– and growing stronger in might
Down mountains of granite and steel
Soon off the cliff; plunging with zeal;
But to observe its force feels surreal

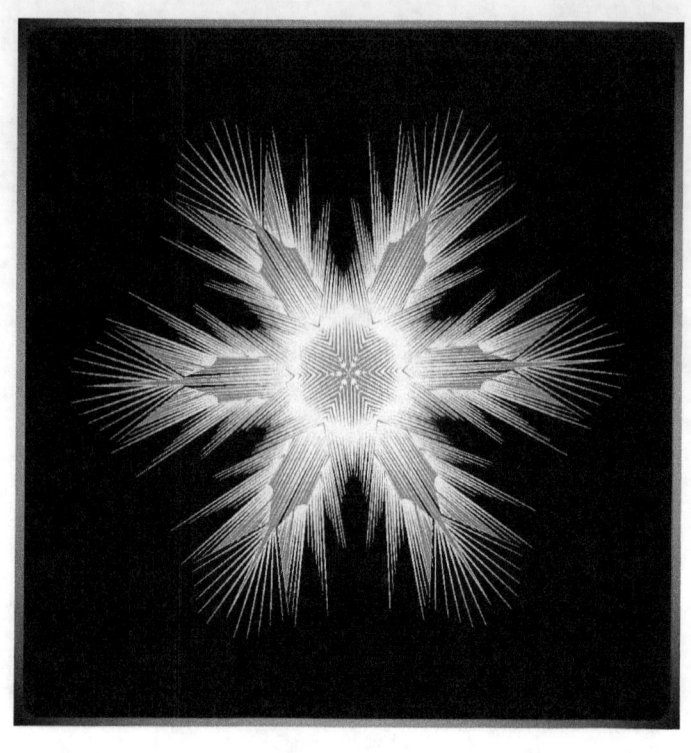

Snow Cone

Crunchy frost covered in wafer-thin syrup
Of fluorescent blueberry or sweet lime
With grape and watermelon- so sublime
In cones of paper; wilting and dripping
Inside giant balls heaped on top of itself
With a rainbow of tiny ice cubes to collide
In a snow cone– messy and soon liquefied

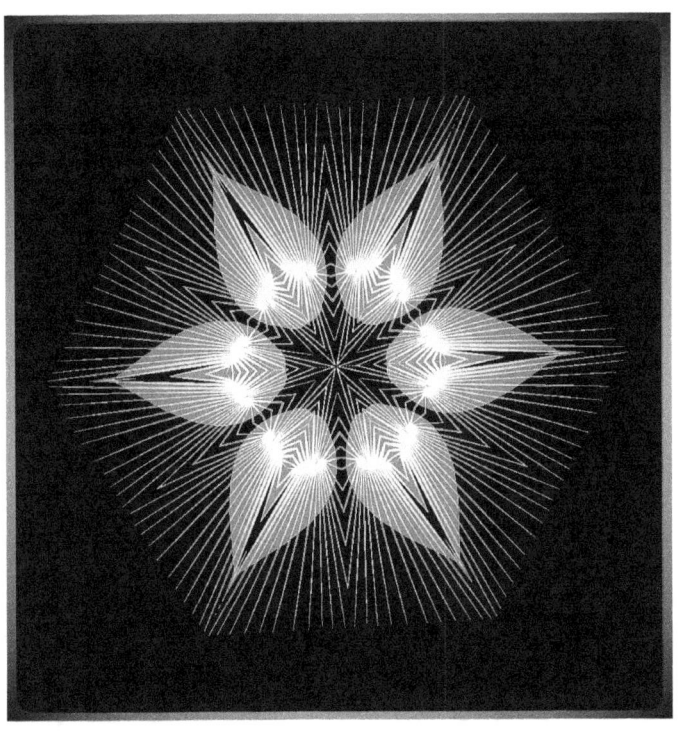

Paper Lanterns

Floating in mist and ascending upward
They connect like a strand of Edison bulbs
Or snowflakes holding hands across the sky
Cut out in wafer thin designs of exotic filament
That fade into pinpricks of flickering light
With dreams to help guide them in their flight

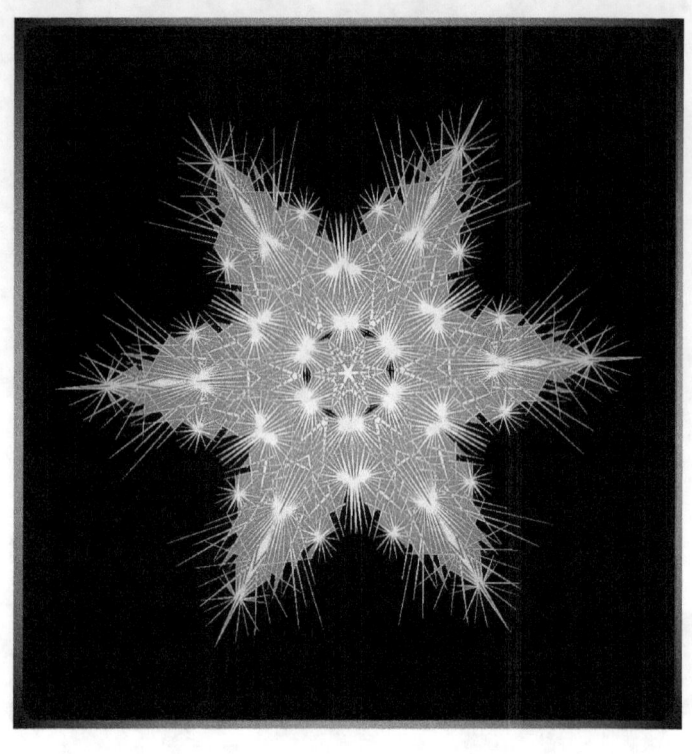

River Freeze

Blue water with crystals; freezing gradually
When stiffening peaks of meringue form
As the river becomes thick with icicles
That hang precariously over cragged rocks
And stalactites of ice break off and thaw
Only to gather and cluster in glass-like luster
That trickles with bubbles caught underneath
Where it holds its breath, until sun melts it again

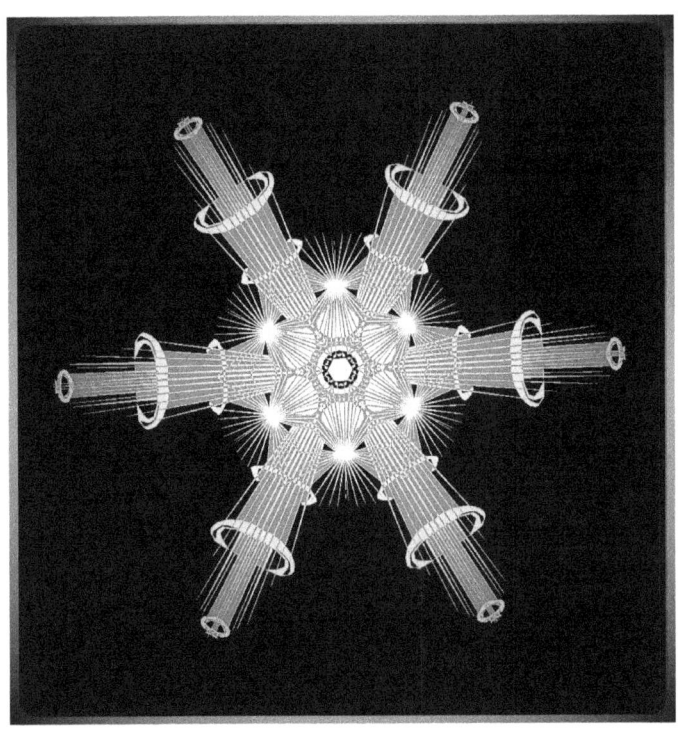

Cut and Erase

Drawing with determination; I make a flake
With ease and temperance— oh, it's a tease
And a steady hand- mouse does as it will please
To cut a flake that soon looks like a disease
Only to delete its form— to cut and erase
Then recut it from scratch and try again
And let my silly flake fall like a masterpiece

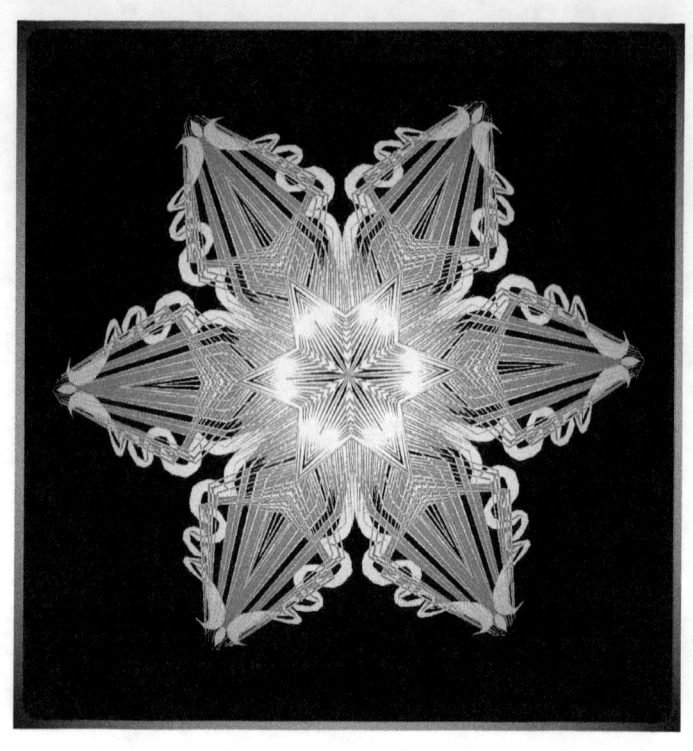

Shattered Glass

Fairy floss weaves in and out of falling snow
Cascading layers of silken tapestry to surround
And freezes brilliant gems with prism's charm
Only to shatter in chaos if touched or worn;
Turning into shards of glass strewn about
As the illusion of mirrors fades in memory
When perfect reflections melt and depart

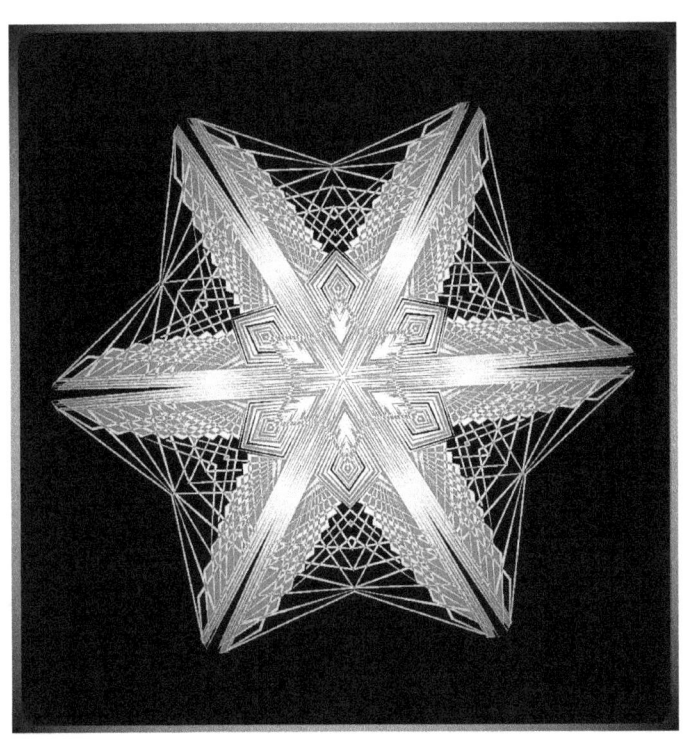

Shy angel

Bashful and shy; she silently glides
Amongst majestic beauty of angels
And thinking she is lesser than them
She folds her arms and blends in
Until eyes of love unfold her wings
As her unique crystal blades shimmer
And revives her grace in brilliant awe

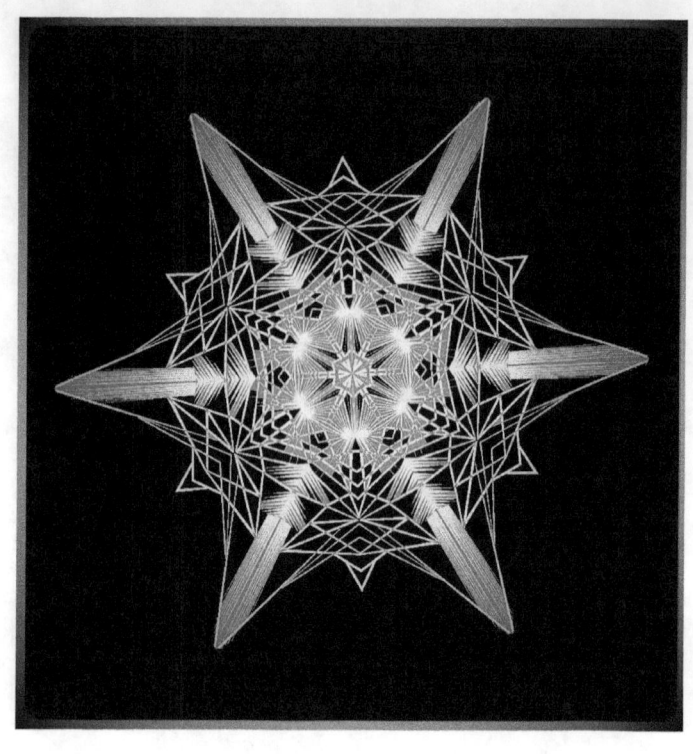

Silent Storms

Fairies carry invisible strands of light
Across tall mountains of ice and snow
With mischief and glee; they dance about
Zapping frozen branches that stiffen,
As shadows of their wings flitter about
When silent storms hide their true form

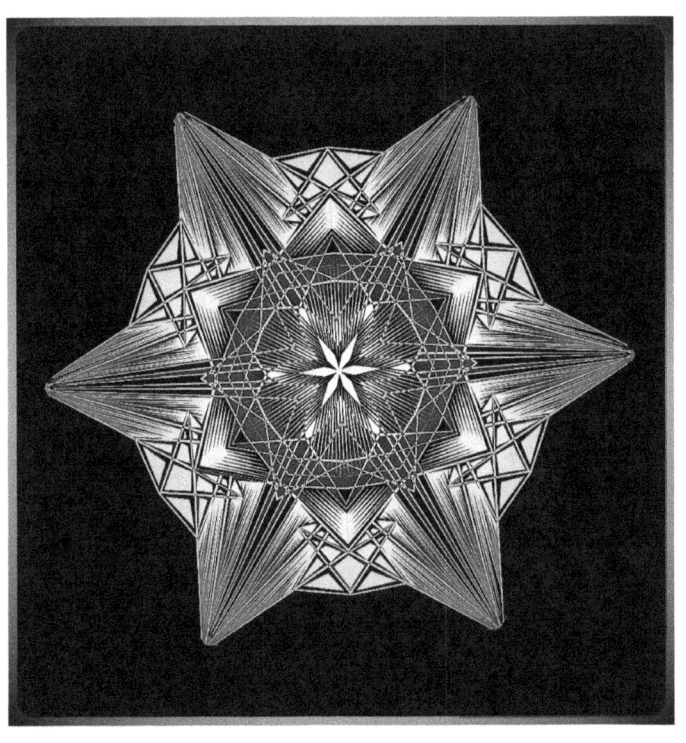

Skate

Gliding on sheets of ice come morn
As sharp metal skids and pirouettes
And trees cuddle around frozen ponds
As nature is quietly watching me skate
To Spirograph my steps in a grant ballet

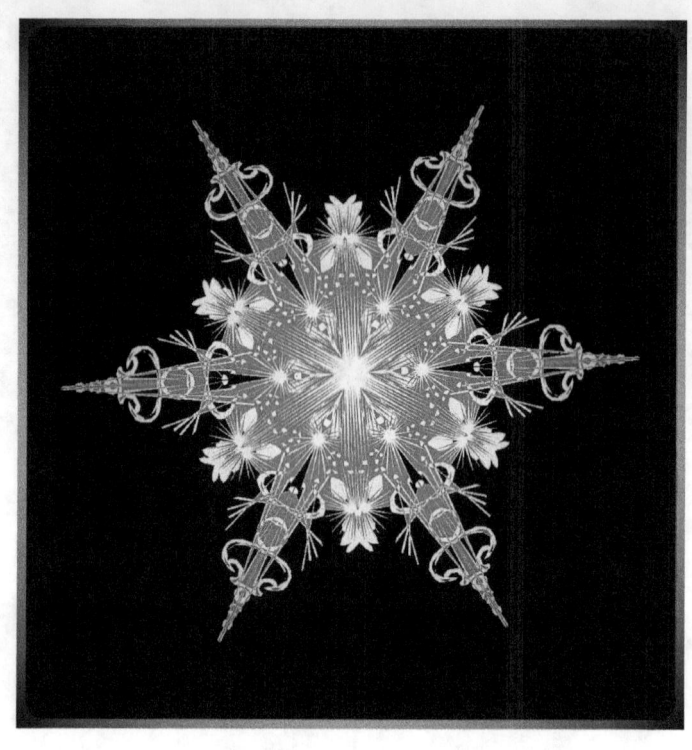

Lighthouse

It stands in tempests and crashing seas
On craggy rocks to support and guide
Shrouded in a blanket of dew in fog
As fingers of lightning crash– and roaring
Ocean drinks in snow from low clouds
And beams from beacon shine like prisms
To warn all who would ride out a storm
As a little mouse guards the lighthouse

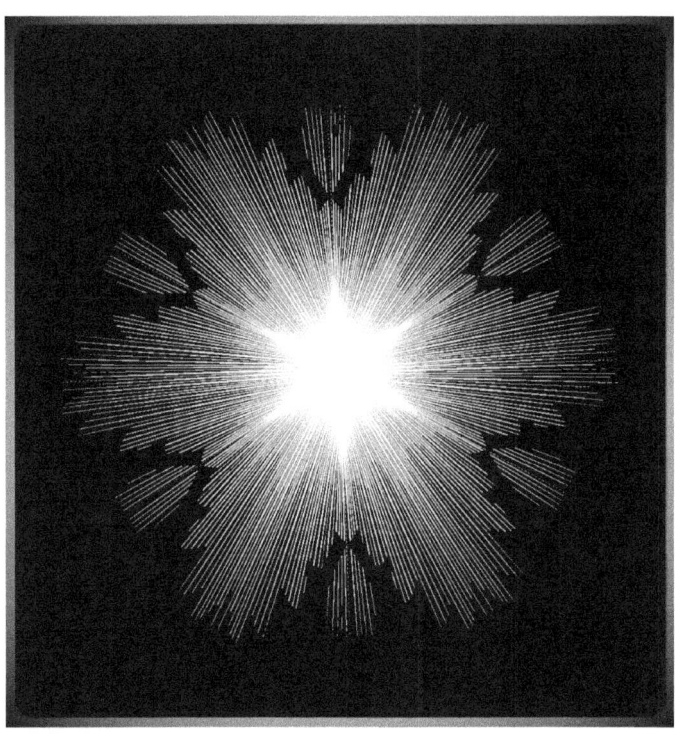

Sleigh

As wind whips on faces chilled with frost
And sleigh wanders down a winding path
Through tall evergreens; thick with snow;
Capping each one with whipped cream,
And kisses from stars shine down below
As valley beyond twinkles ever so bright
In a welcoming sight to guide us home

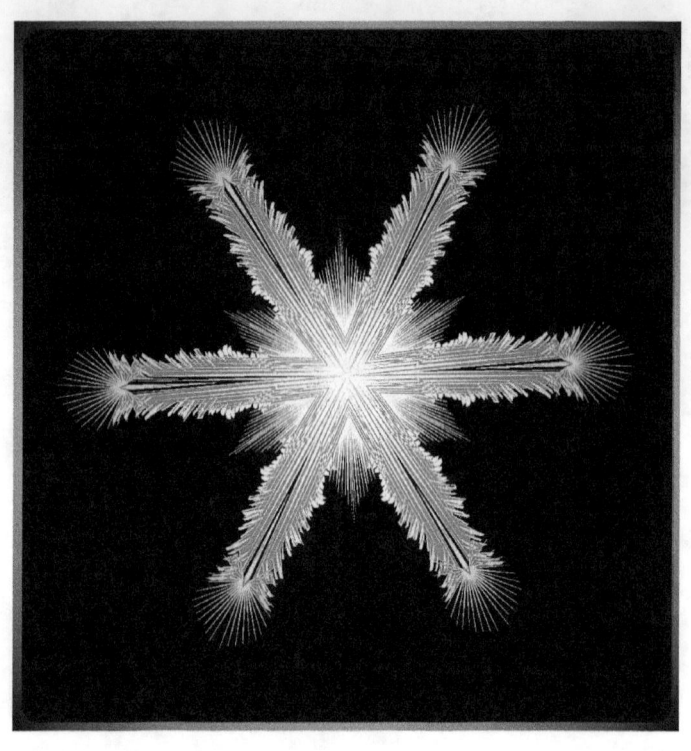

Icicles

Beaded water hanging over fences and roofs
Gliding into jagged daggers and freezing rain
Like spears of pointed quartz or selenite wands
They embrace heat and cool; growing slowly
To become a formidable fortress all their own
And as sun coaxes them out; they fall down
And break apart into cold puddles of water

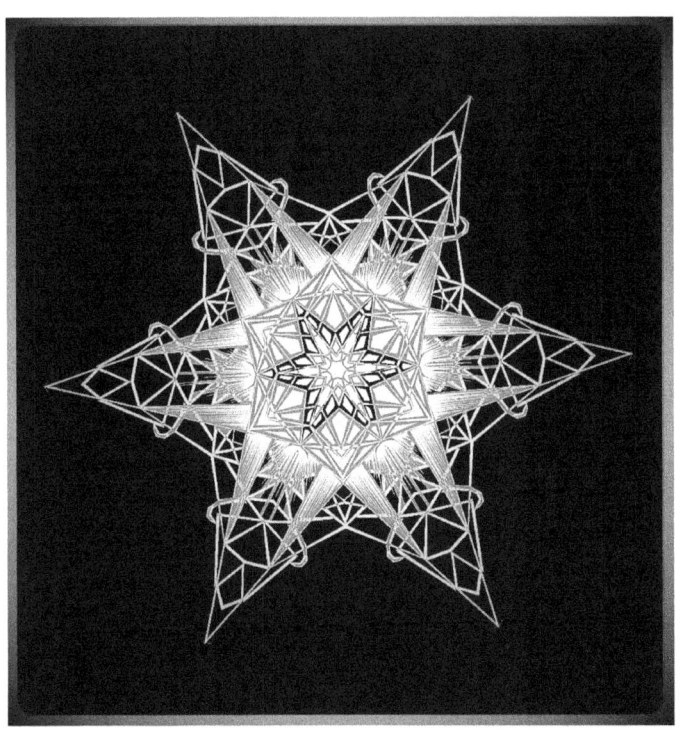

Snow Prayer

When flakes fall like tiny shooting stars
And each one is blessed and complete;
I know they came from heaven above
When I pray for cold, snowy weather
As I stand outside in solemn wonder
Looking to the sky in sweet surrender

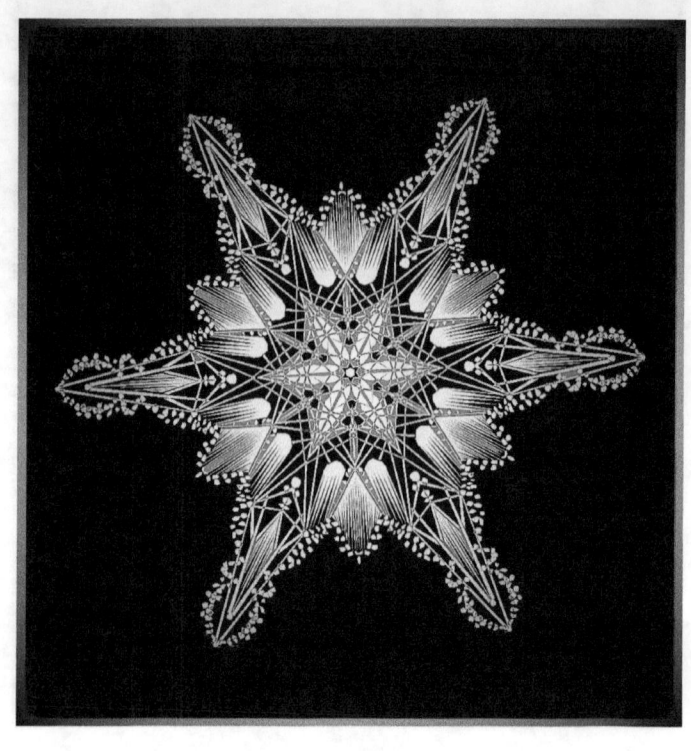

Snowdrop Petals

If breath falls on snowdrop petals
Then magic blossoms with ease–
Freshly fallen; yet brittle and clear
Like berries blushing in icy retreat
Where frost shivers on faded dreams
And sweet crème brûlée splatters about
In lucid thought- colliding with crystals
As snowflakes bend with glittery sheen

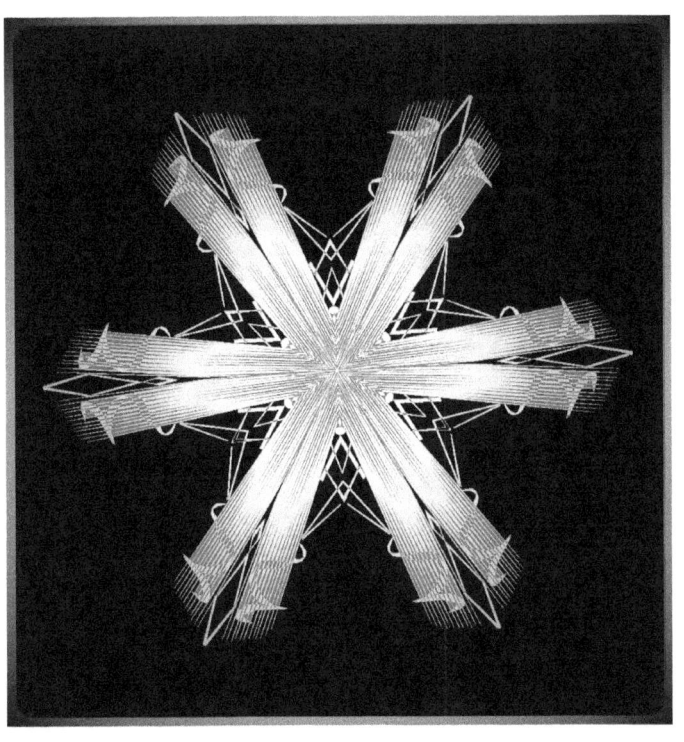

My Flakes

Quietly scribbling flakes late at night;
Making little cuts in a white filigree
To add beauty and a trace of elegance
Or chaos circled in a hot mess– I guess
But love it or hate it; I am relieved
When my flakes glow with love and sass
And stamp them with a touch of class

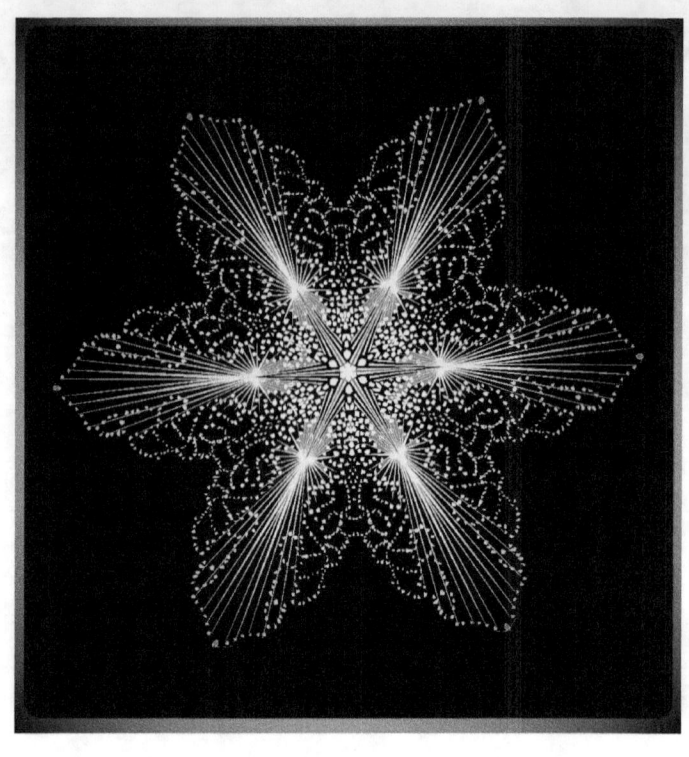

Glowing Moon

Luminous strands of gauze shimmer on snow
With fire opals and obsidian spreading like stars
As dust filled beams sweep across silver galaxies
Falling through space and gently casting its glow
Where clouds surround and bathe in soft light
As moon watches all creatures during the night

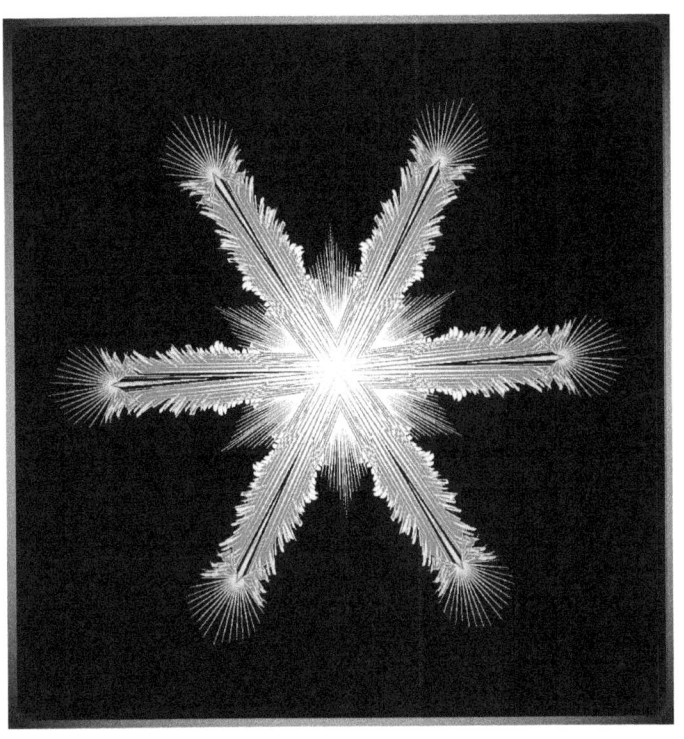

Frost

Crackling and growing without a sound
It forms like a cluster with crystals of snow
With luminous slivers that cause all to shiver
As it seeps in and out of autumn's weather
And into winter with thickened intent–
To blanket and chill, until springtime is sent

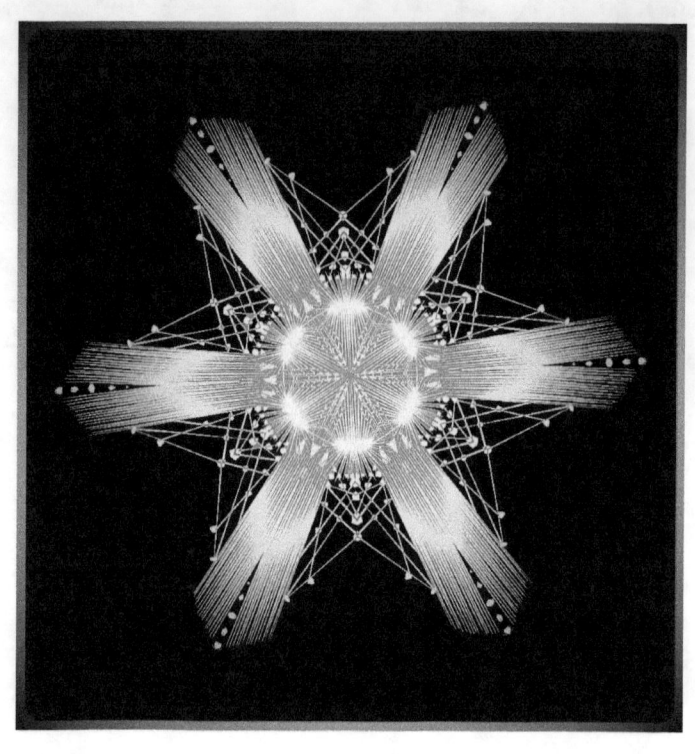

Coffee

Marshmallow snowflakes in coffee;
Swirled around
That dance and shiver; spiced with nutmeg
Steaming with hot cocoa and melting in heat
Now dancing and coalescing for a tasty treat

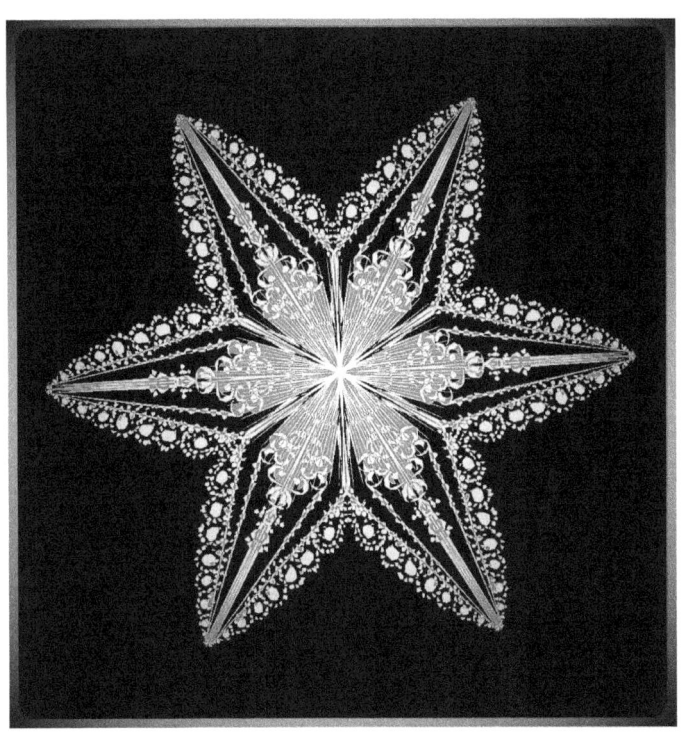

Berries of Gold

Frosting sprays on berries of gold
Hanging off tree limbs bare of leaves
Where dew catches and gently freezes
Dripping down and hardening in cold
Across icy fields white with soft folds

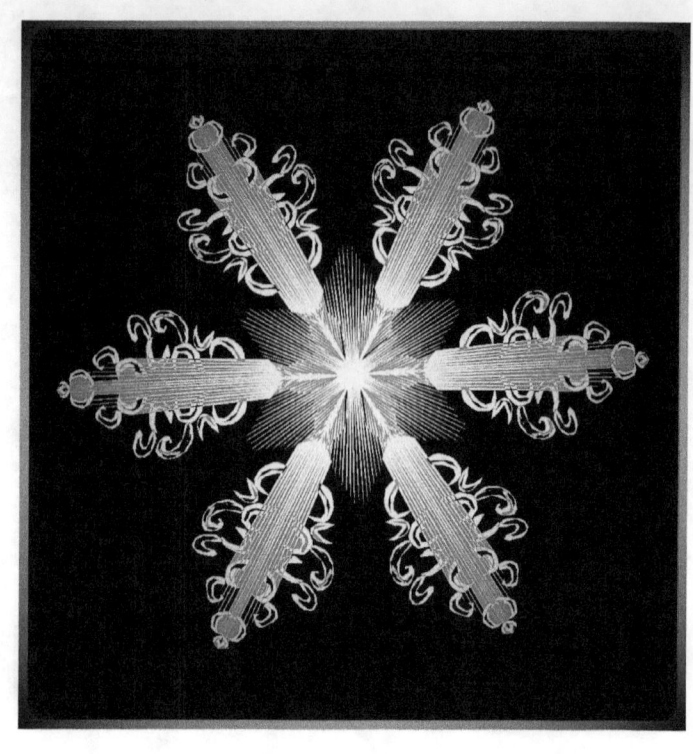

Ugly flake

If an ugly flake could talk to you;
Would it ask you to love it true?
And parade on streets and strut about;
Wearing bows and fur in grand aplomb?
But if I could talk to you– dear ugly flake
I would say to stop trying so hard;
For no flake is ugly, unless you say it's true
Because all flakes are flawed- I say to you

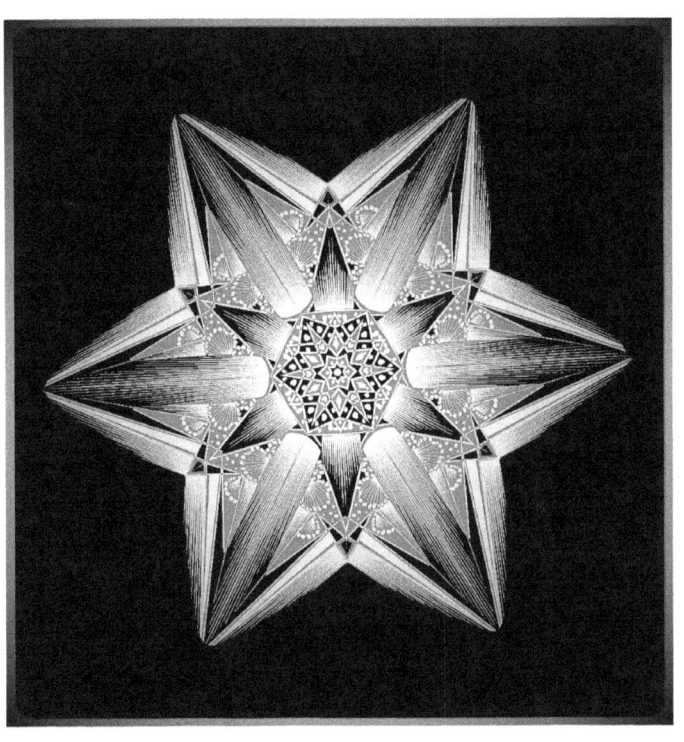

Winter's Song

Pinecones dipped in icing and frosted glass
With tart berries frozen in icicle fondant
That scatter on ground with icy embrace
As branches of trees dip low with heaviness
When snow nestles in needles of spruce
And wind blows with a song all its own
That calls to any who will listen to its cry
As sweet slumber cocoons forest in song

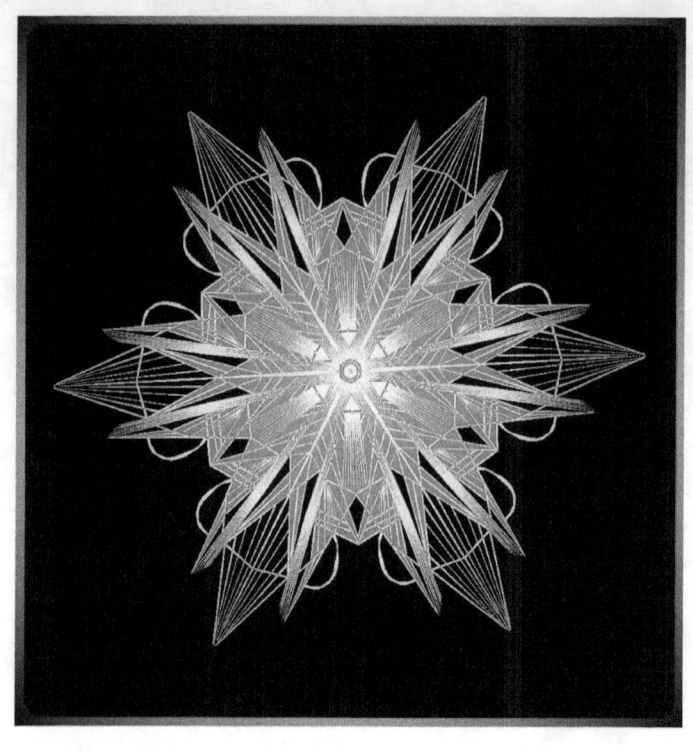

Tree Topper

On top of a decked-out Christmas tree
In brilliant colors of ornaments spun
Is a Star of Bethlehem of festive wonder,
Or a dazzling angel guarding with her arms
By sacred candlelight and tinseled charms
In nostalgic glitter's glow- when days are cold
And memories weave in and out of light
Where awe and love can still be found

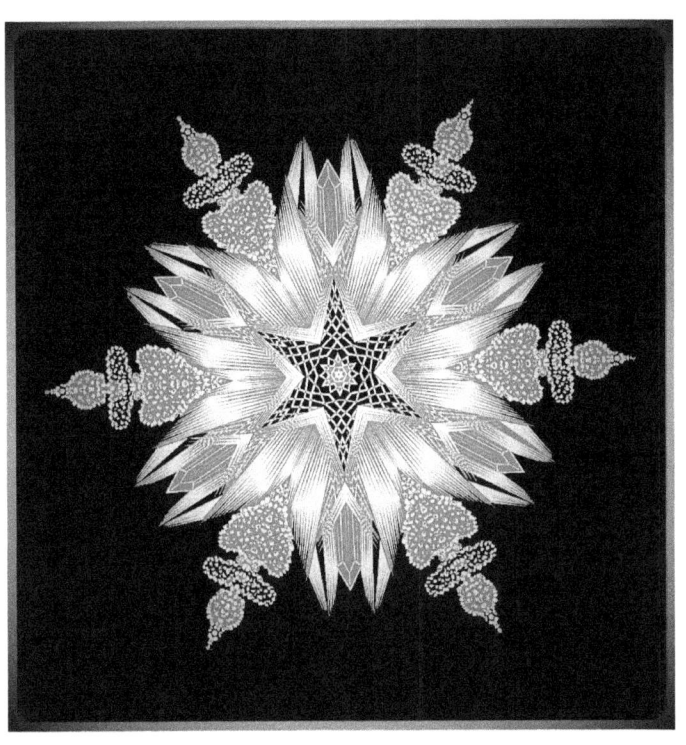

Snowgarden of the Queen

Elves bundle each one carefully by hand
To decorate frozen canopies of ice
And guard them in the palace of snow
Where all are on display for regal queen,
As enchantments of winter keep them safe
Forever encased in an icy wonderland
Where dreams and magic spellbind to hide
All wishes; now in twilight's delicate sheen

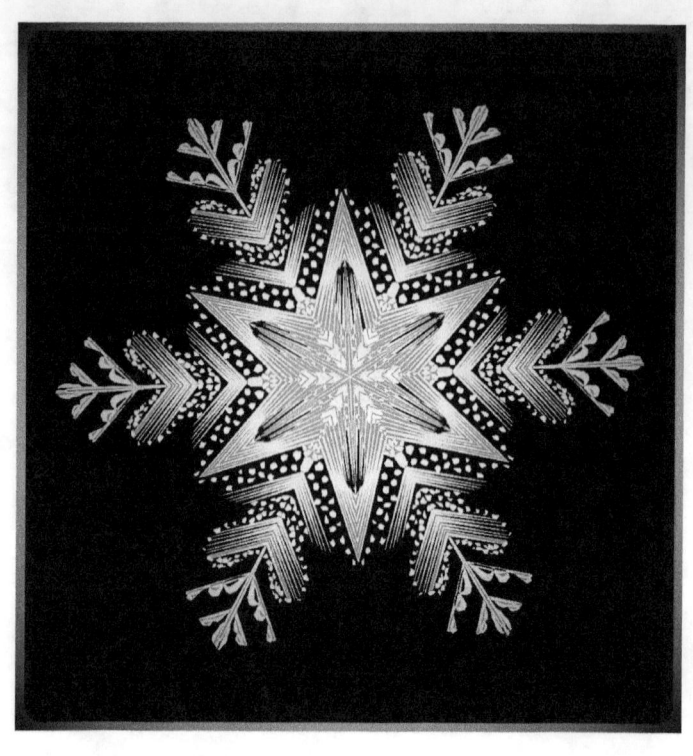

Reindeer

Specks of dust in crystalline vistas
Veiled from view and coming closer
With antlers like brambles in a thicket
Are reindeer with undercoats of velvet
That watch over their young in tundra
And play and jostle in the middle of winter

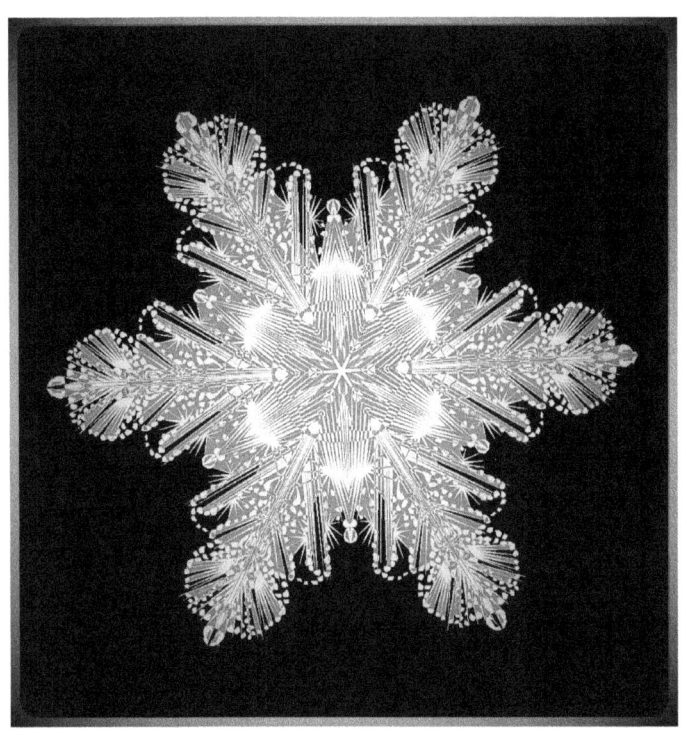

Bells

Frosted metal of blueberries in sugar
Coating heavy steel with swaying balls
That hide inside towers of ancient tolls;
And sounds at midnight in arching steeples
Are bells of Christmas to bid thee well

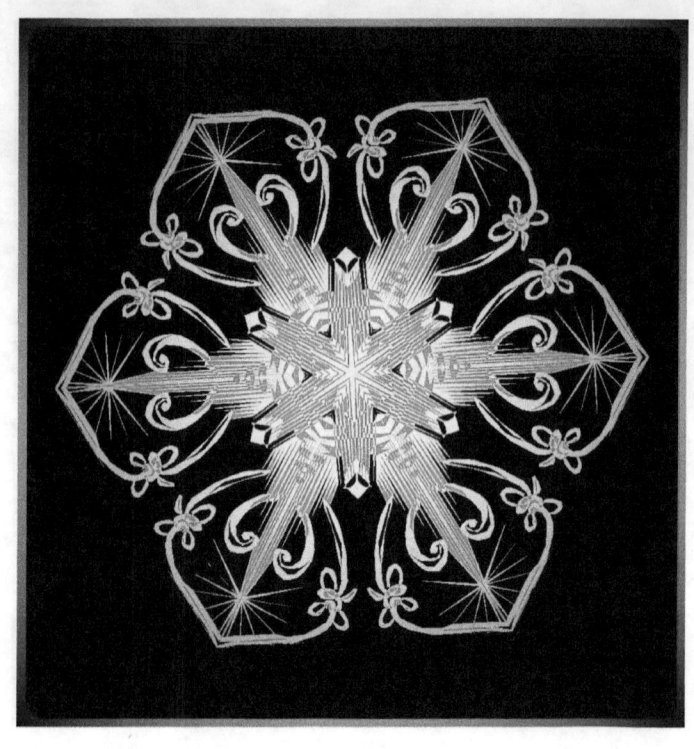

Ice Castle

In sheerest glass of iridescent filament
Is a castle of wonder with towered icicles
That pierce eggshell blue sky in brilliance
While doors of frigid cold block out heat
And chill of arctic magic reflects icy prisms
As winter sun preserves it in true form

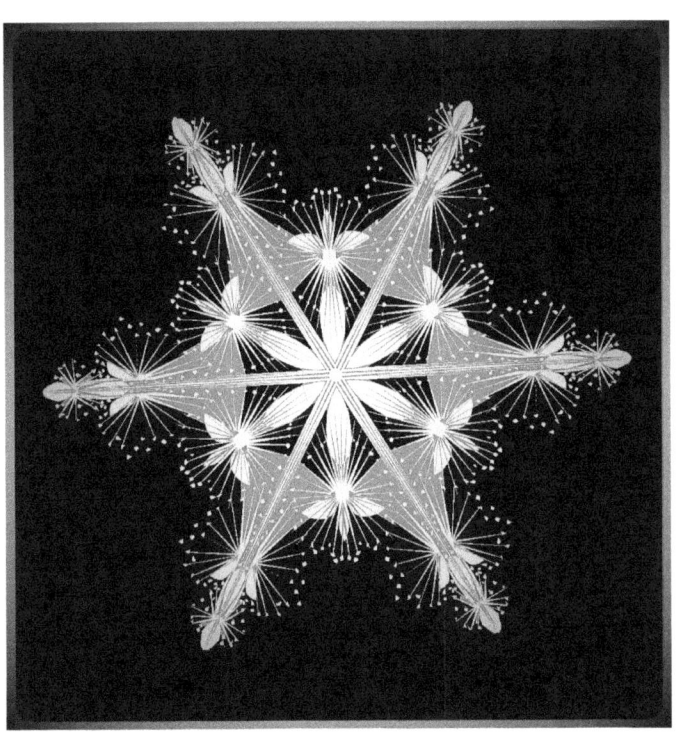

Winter Solstice

Embracing dark and letting go of day
Swaying back and forth; when sun retreats
As night holds hands across evening sky
To follow paths of centuries gone by
Towards winter's grip and all grows cold
When winter solstice arrives in dark display

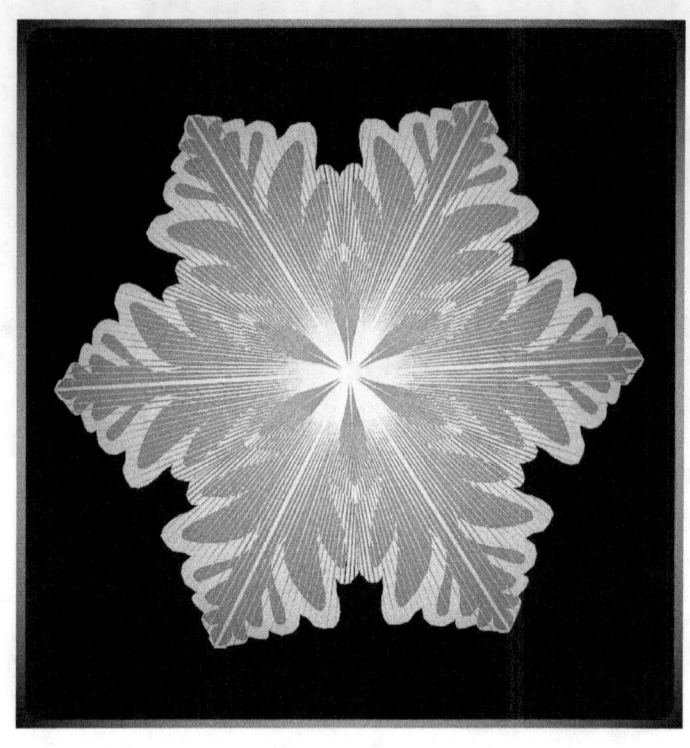

Iceberg

Crushed daquiri ice of purest blue
Like aquamarine and topaz shards
Sipping on liquid fissures of snow
And quietly shedding flecks in a fury
Is an iceberg submerged deep below

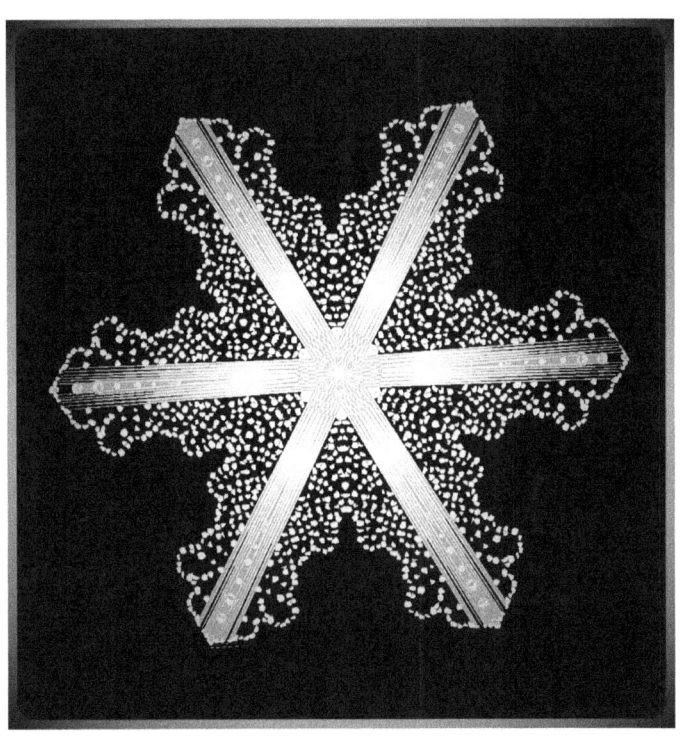

Balls of Snow

Craters of slush crushed from snow
Like thudding hail; it clumps about
And feathers of frost spread on grass
While circles of clouds swipe around
As balls of snow bounce on the ground

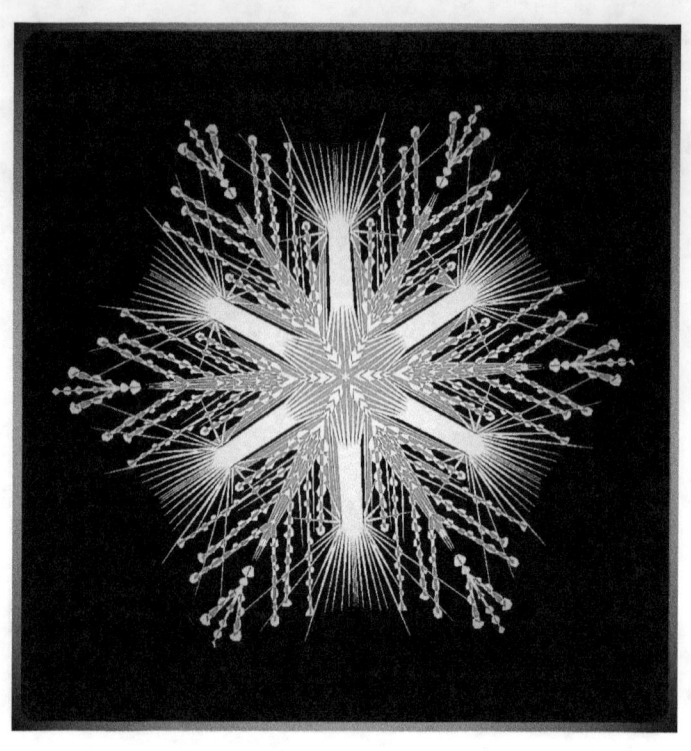

Silence

As snow falls and silence fills the air
And sweet smell of cold is ever clear
When fauna stops and life takes a pause
As nature unleashes inclement weather
To blanket all in her lacey winter gauze

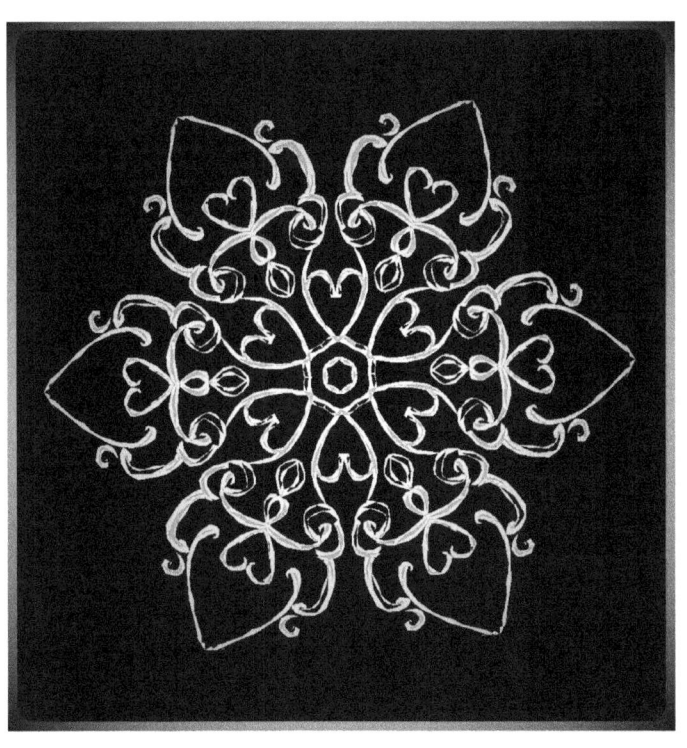

Thaw my heart

If love was a tattered snowflake
Worn and weary from life's storms
Falling past all hope to evaporate;
I remember your charm and wit
Yet when I try to love you again;
You blow hot and cold like a flake
And make me want to finally quit
But thaw my heart- I still want it!

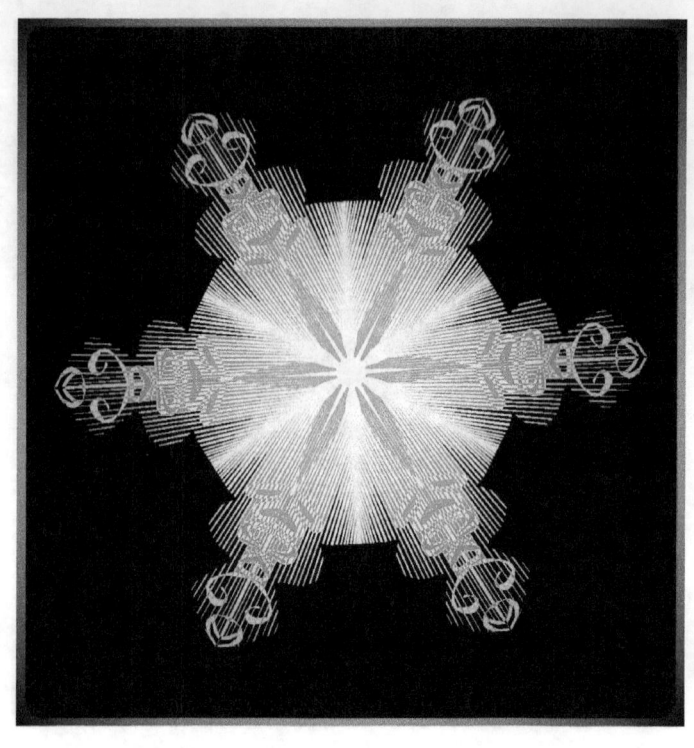

Snow Woman

If stories told the truth indeed
They would know that he's a she—
Plump and stout, without a doubt,
But full of laughter and a sneeze—
Amused and playing as she grows;
This snow woman is a frosty tease

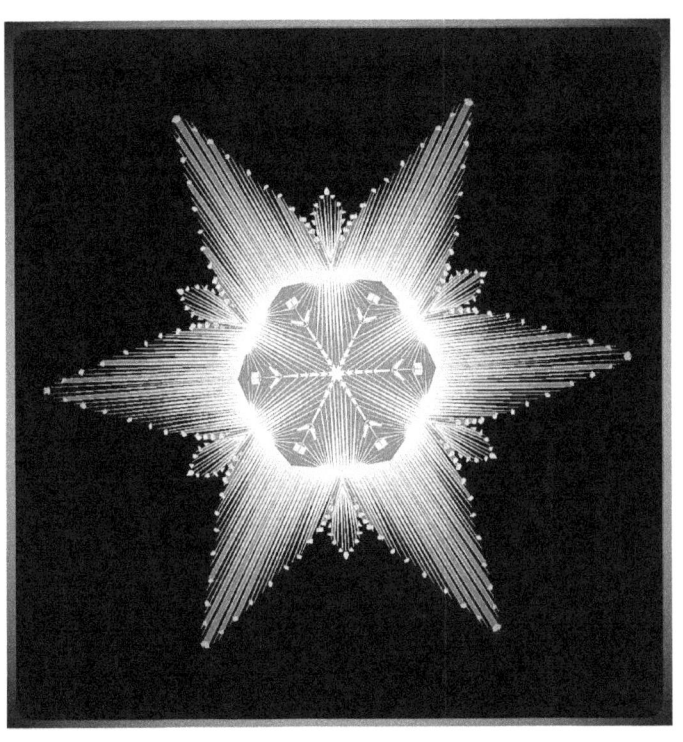

Littlest snowflake

Waning between shadows and light
Lies a snowflake cold with fright
And embedding in a bubble of ice
Barely seen, as it twinkles just so–
Tangled in frothy spindles of sleet
Nestling between morning and night

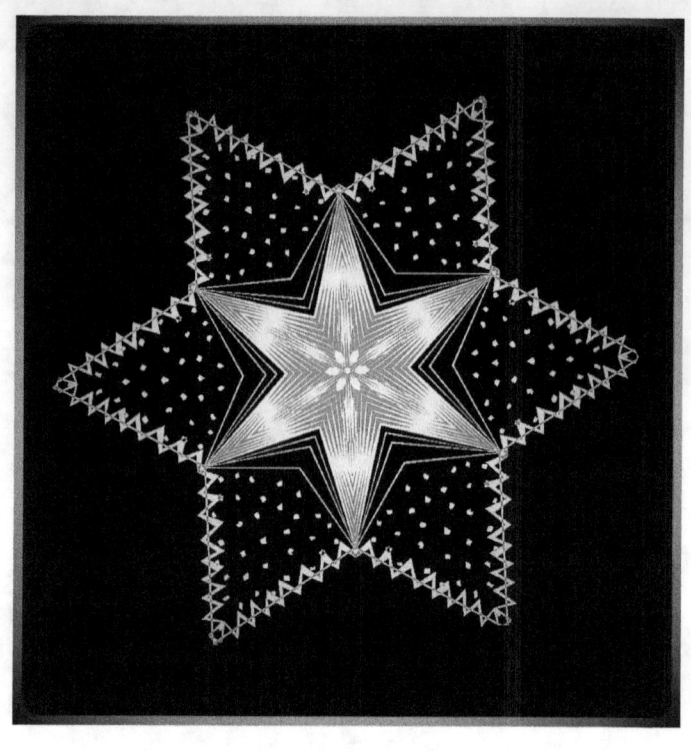

That Scarf

Winding in circles and coiled tight
Like petals of roses not yet in bloom
Then snagging on twigs and branches
That muffles my breath and cocoons–
Is a red scarf that unravels all too soon

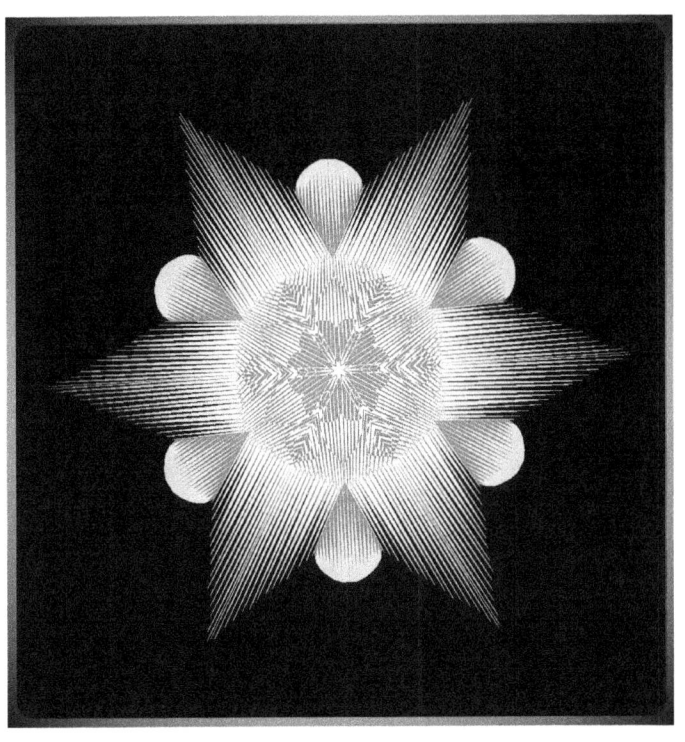

Snow House

Clear ice cubes of frigid snow and sugar
With thin icicles frozen between bricks
Of a canopy- like a chandelier in frost
That towers and glows with light inside;
Illuminating softly all over the countryside

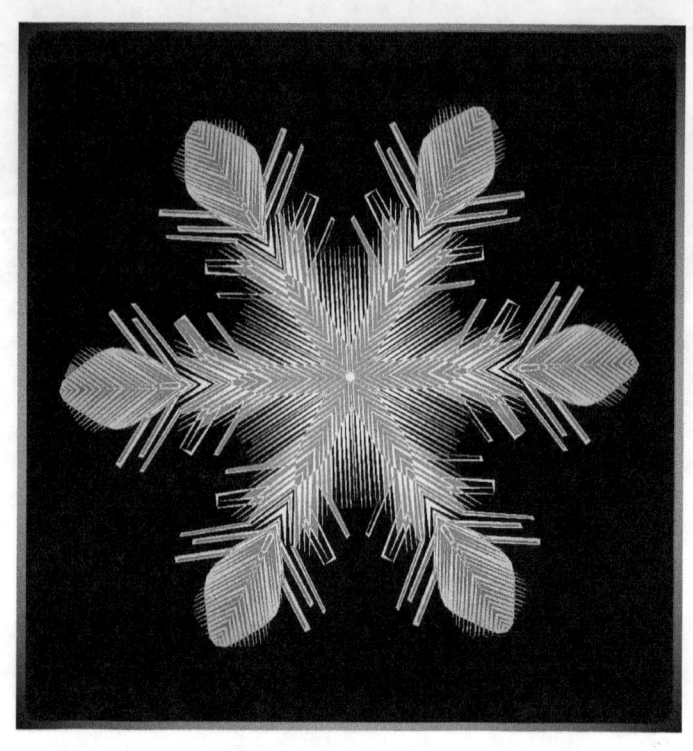

Candy twists

Crushed silver dragees in peppermint mist
And caramels twisting with hazelnut kisses
That tumble from stockings hung with care
And chocolate stars spin in golden frost
With snowflake buttercream that falls apart
To sweeten holidays with love from the start

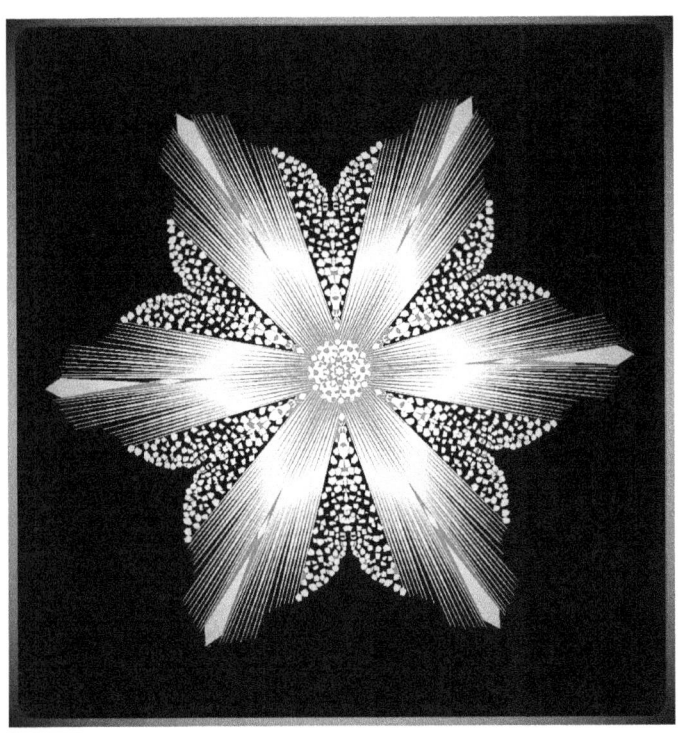

Lake in winter

Like a flat mirror of molten silver
Grasping its fingers towards daylight
With sleek skin to cover liquid below–
And thicken, but cracks and refreezes
With fissures forming in frigid pieces
To skate on its shell of frozen layers
Is frosty magic of a lake in winter

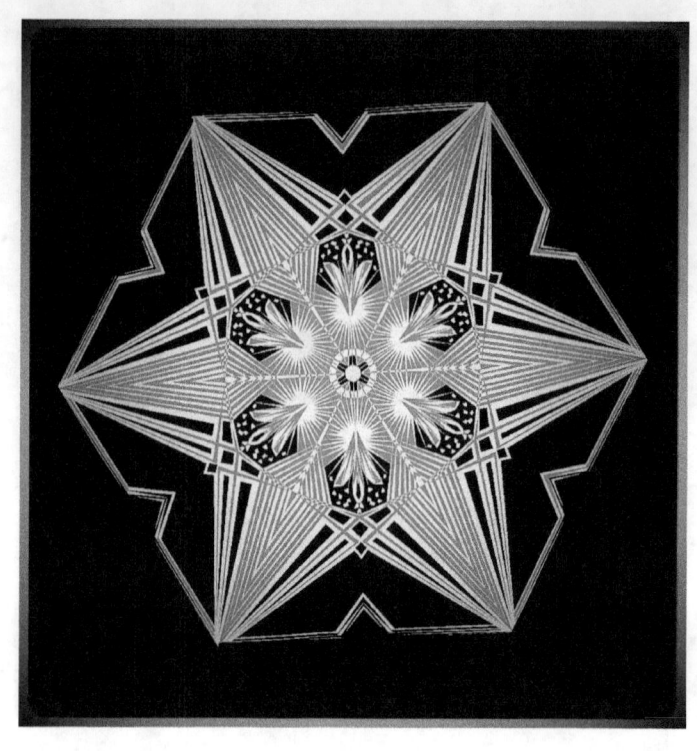

Elven art

Snip and cut- they shatter apart
As elves decorate falling snowflakes
And gather strands to craft their art
With blades made from ice and frost–
They spin floss– weaving in and out
To make snowflakes glow with luster
And fall from clouds during winter

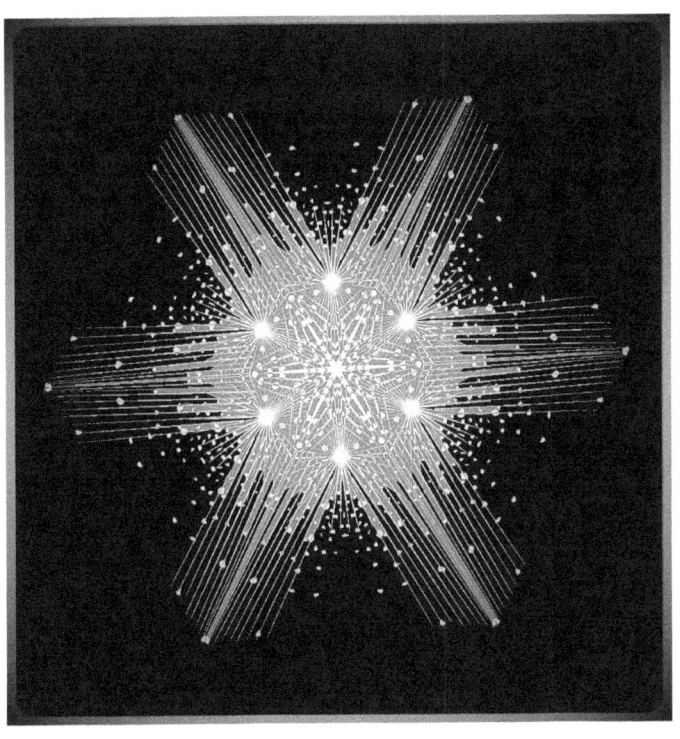

Northern Lights

Fire floats at night with gossamer gowns
Of blue and green curling in wisps
That caress stars and moon in twilight
As Artic breeze with pillars from heaven
Hovers in strands of swiping paint;
Smearing across canvas of land and snow
As northern lights cast their eerie glow

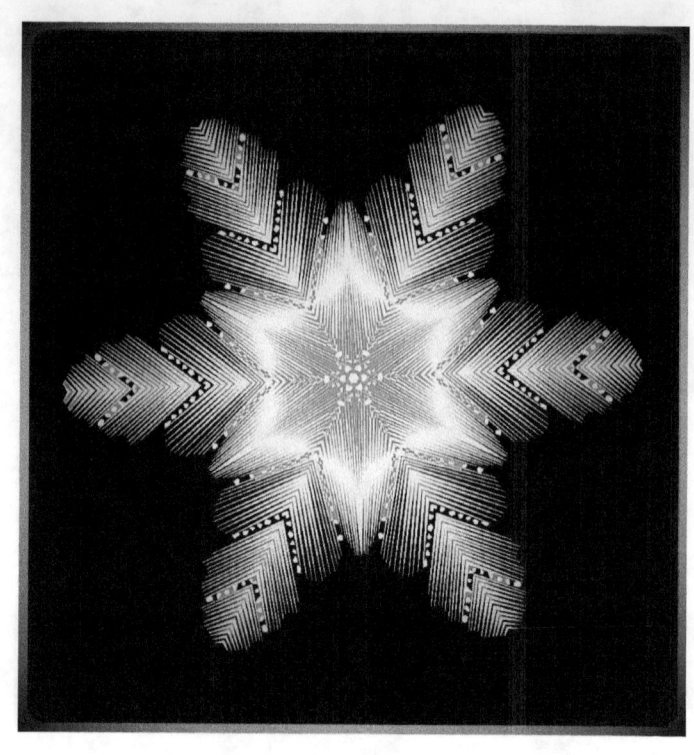

holiday cookies

Butter and flour with sugar and spice
Making Christmas cookies twice as nice
And some decorated with lemony zest
That melts like snowflakes in your mouth
As grandma bakes her holiday best

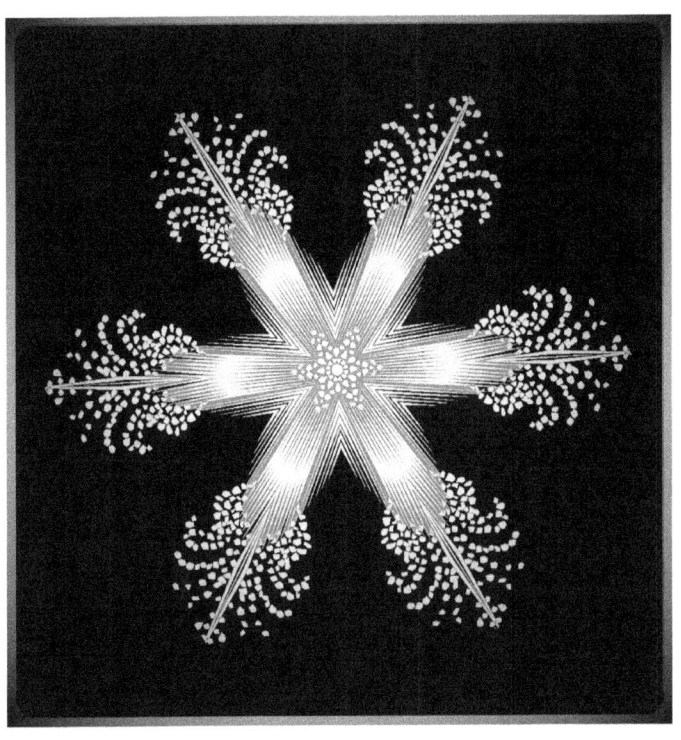

Ivy and Holly

Greenery draped on wooden staircases
Twirled around like a garland of spruce
With red berries tangled together–
Holding hands like gingerbread cutouts
And spiraling over fireplaces and walls
When ivy and holly decorate for yuletide
That brings winter's design in grand halls

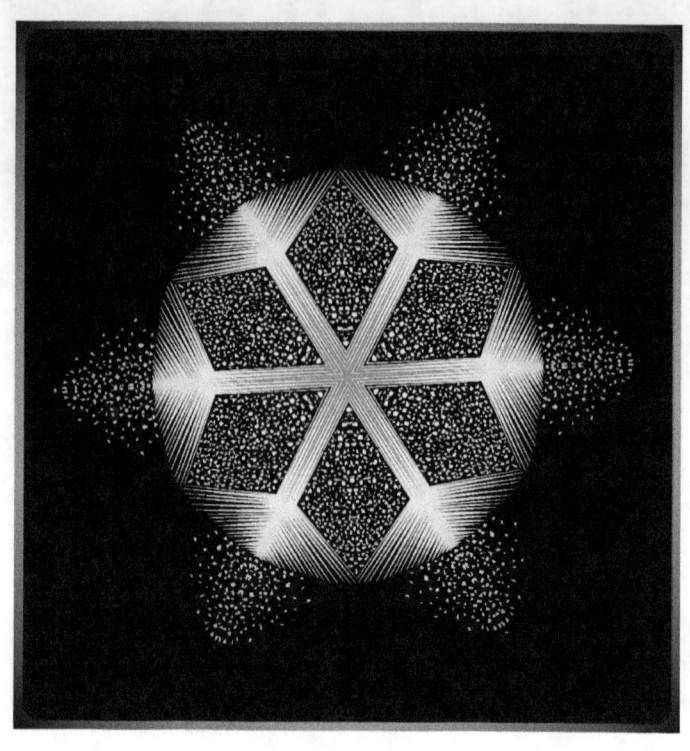

Windowpane

Gentle snow falls like powdered sugar
Coating my windowpane in December
And melting as it lands on cold glass
But soon freezes in an arctic blast

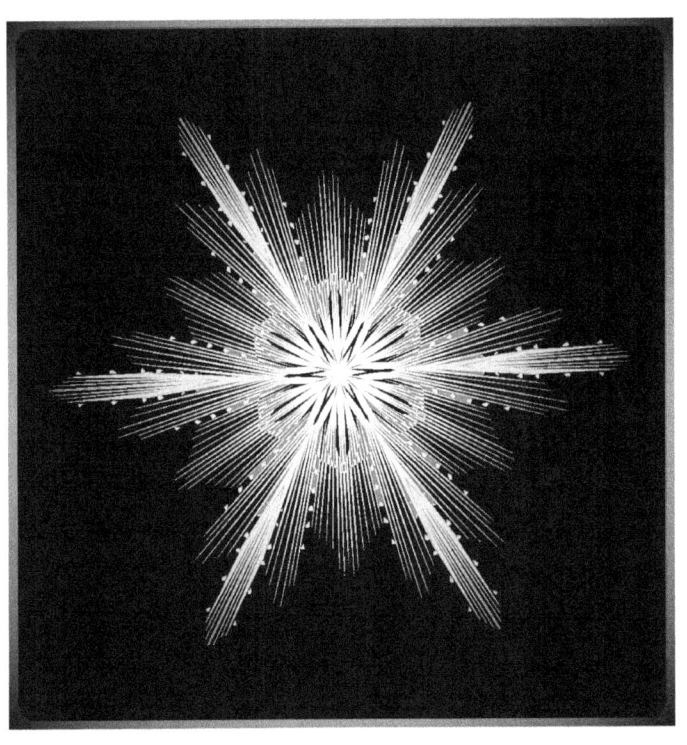

Kris Kringle

Kris Kringle comes with the Christkind
On Christmas Eve in the freezing cold
To deliver toys for good boys and girls
But the next day when gifts are opened
I sometimes wish I was still five years old

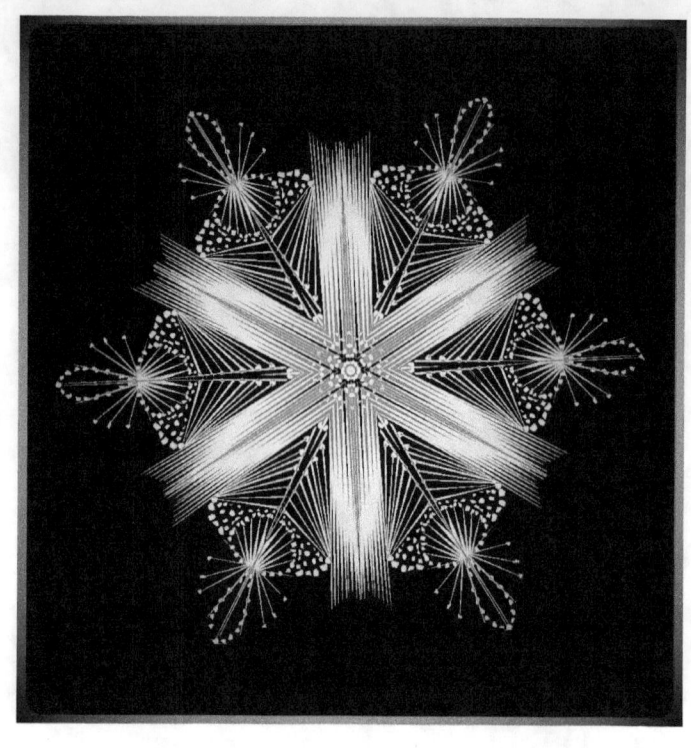

Wreath

Sparkles and stars with evergreen bows
Twisted tightly with a spray of berries
In frosted snow petals with white fondant
And pinecones cling to ribbony film
That twinkle with a spattering of lights
Twirled in circles like a spiral galaxy
As a wreath of Christmas hangs bright

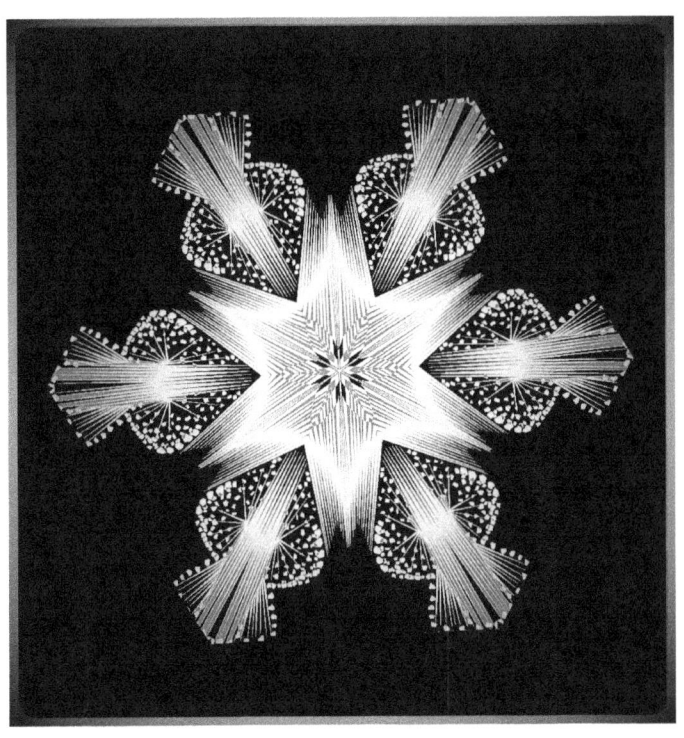

Noel

If the first day of Christmas was a light
Then all month long it grows bright
As yuletide sweeps past autumn's chill
And a star shines with winter's Noel
As wise men travel through the snow
To birth a festive season with its carol

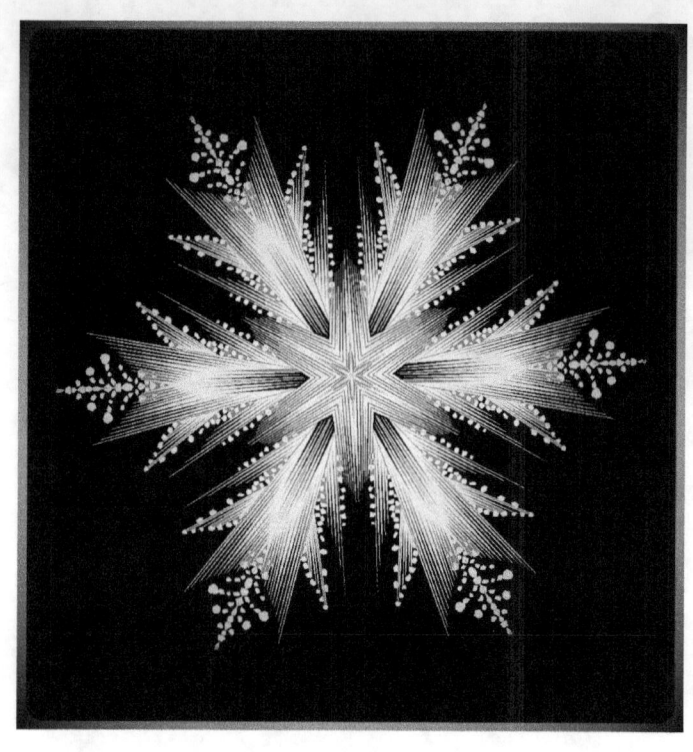

Old Man Winter

With a wand made from sharp icicles
He sprays chilly earth with dendrites
To freeze on hoary trees and clouds
As he watches in his wintery gown
Made from iridescent pearls in foam
And a crown of stars on his head
As Old Man Winter shivers the ground

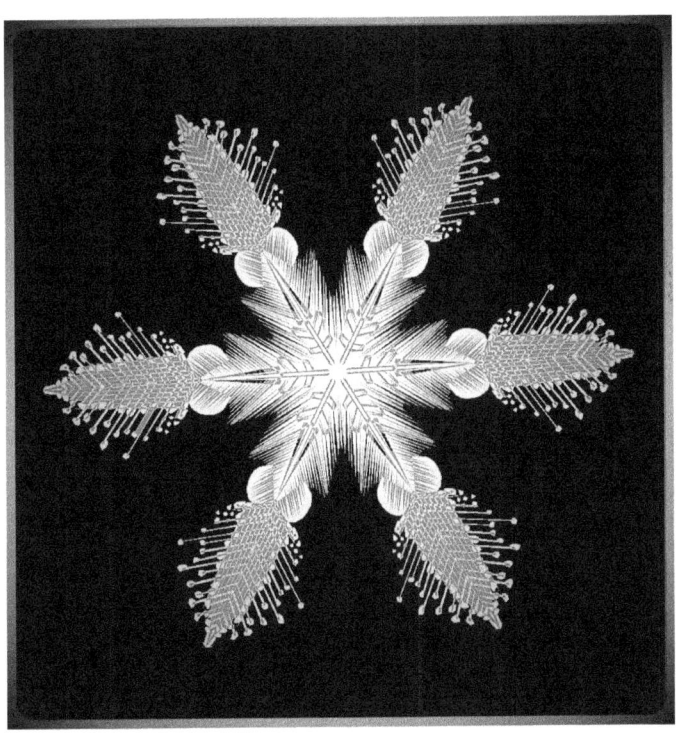

Pinecones

As wind howls through glazed trees
And winter sheds her fine needles
Pinecones scatter on forest floors
When sun shrugs behind frozen hills
To cast light cascading through leaves
As ornaments are strewn on forest floors

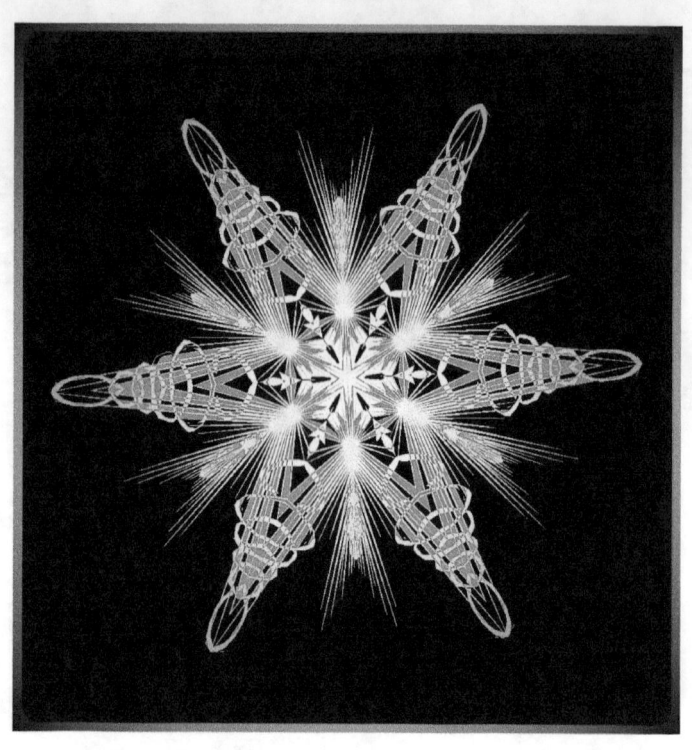

Carolers

With lanterns and hymnals in hand
At doorways when notes will stream
In whispers of breath in icy wind
To fly upon wings of angelic hosts
Are carolers singing nostalgic songs

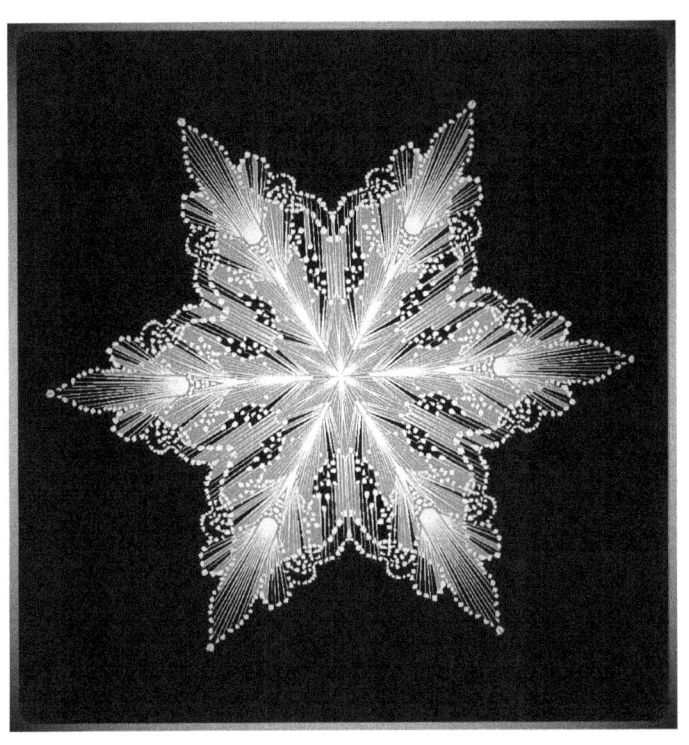

Stained Glass

High above alpine snow; it towers tall
As filtered light falls in quatrefoil prisms
Cascading through kaleidoscope panes
As rainbow symphonies floating in seas
Of stained glass in a medieval castle
Where echoes reverberate in chambers
That inspire all with painted fairy tales

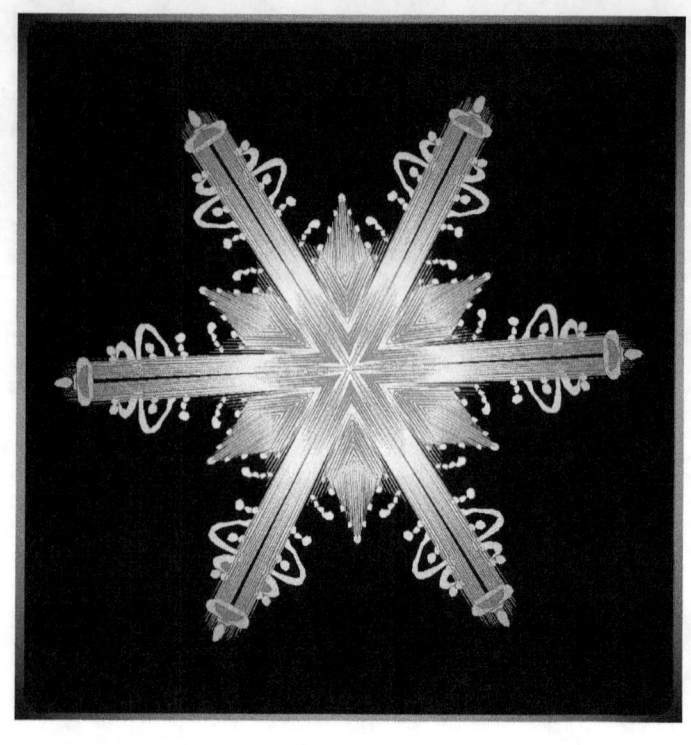

First Snow

In anticipation of winter's first snow
Watching clouds fill with grey light
And fading towards earth- it comes
Like silken fog floating to the ground
And flakes like soggy paper swirl–
Huge, and full of hope that it stays
Until it buries everything for days

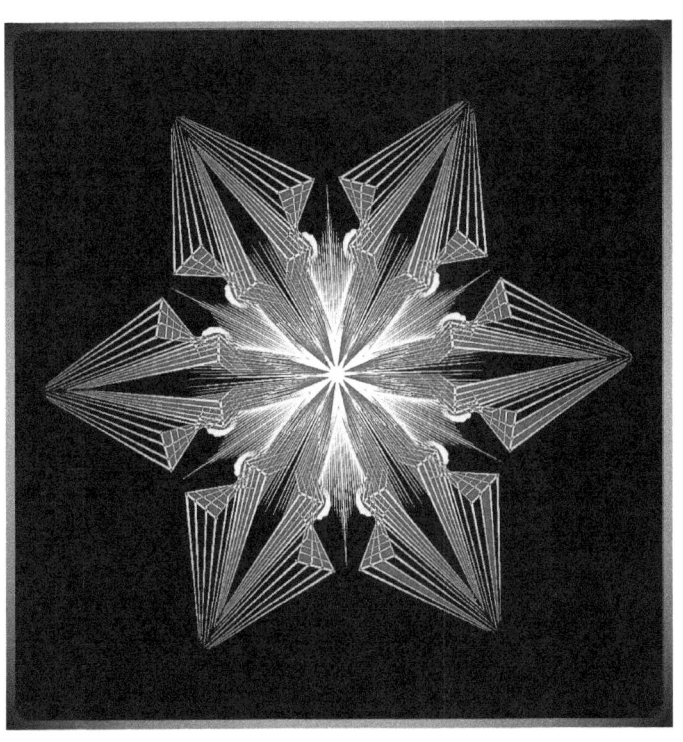

New Year

When midnight tolls and revelries ring
And wishes are made in songs we sing
As fireworks burst with positive kisses
A page unfolds with unwritten words
To start over when a new year is born

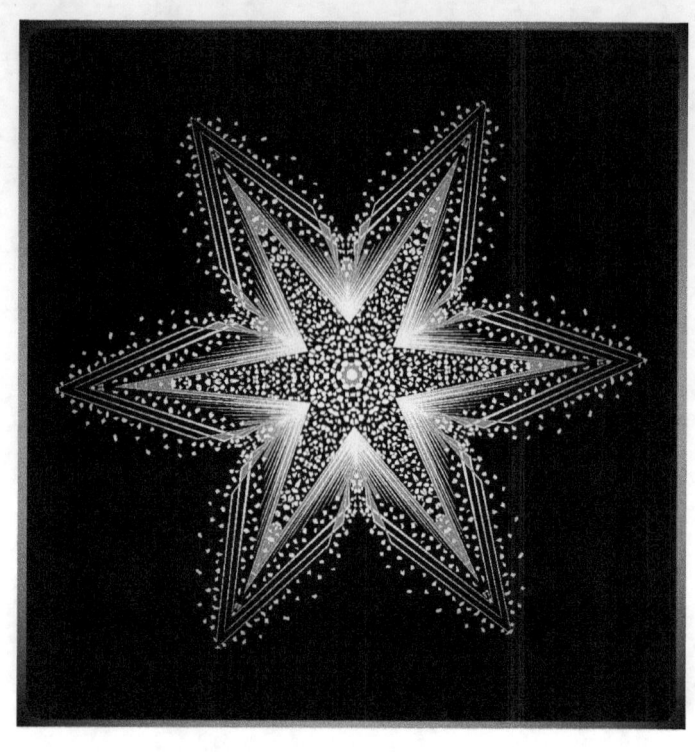

Mele Kalikimaka

In an isle of sand and ocean breezes
Santa comes to say Mele Kalikimaka
Full of sweet presents and tropical treats
And white plumeria blossoms fall about
Like snowflakes that scatter and melt
While orchids woven in purple garlands
Sway at Christmastime in balmy heat

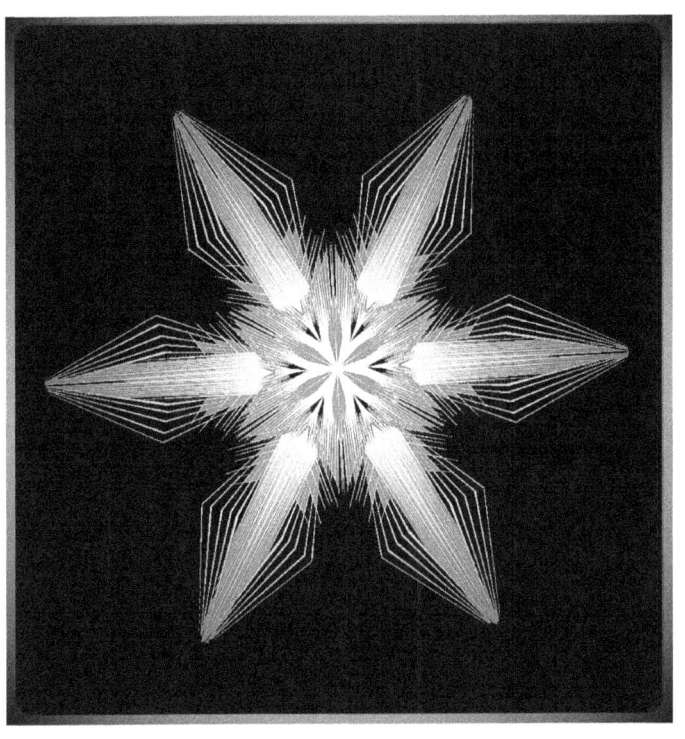

Festival of Lights

Twinkling sparks of pinpricks strung
Across sleepy horizon in twilight dim
In a dazzling show of filament glow
Pulsating colors like broken sea glass
Mesmerizing like an electric rainbow

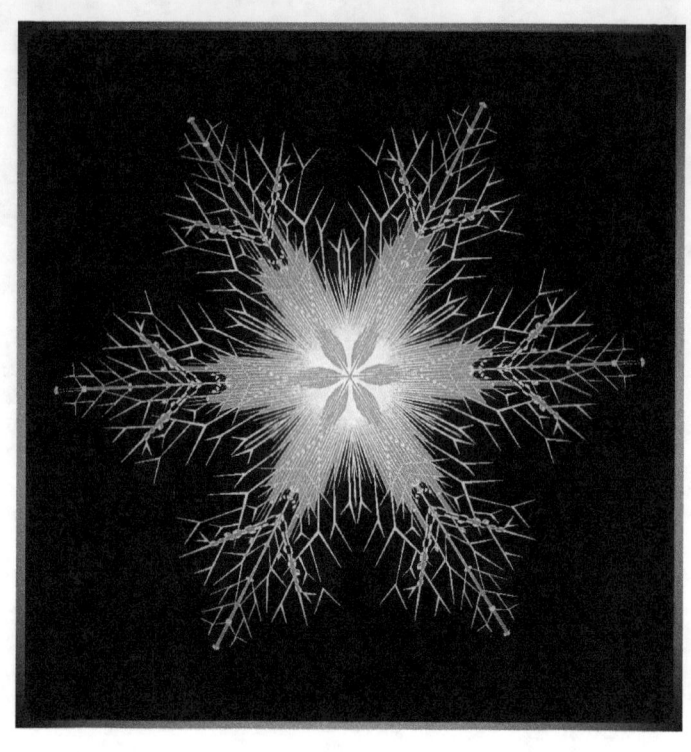

Gingerbread House

Slabs of thick gingerbread bricks
Spackling cracks with white frosting
Dripping icicles on confection sheets
Pelted with bursts of carnival candy
Sprinkled on top like falling snow
Until it looks good enough to eat
But meant for one's eyes as a treat

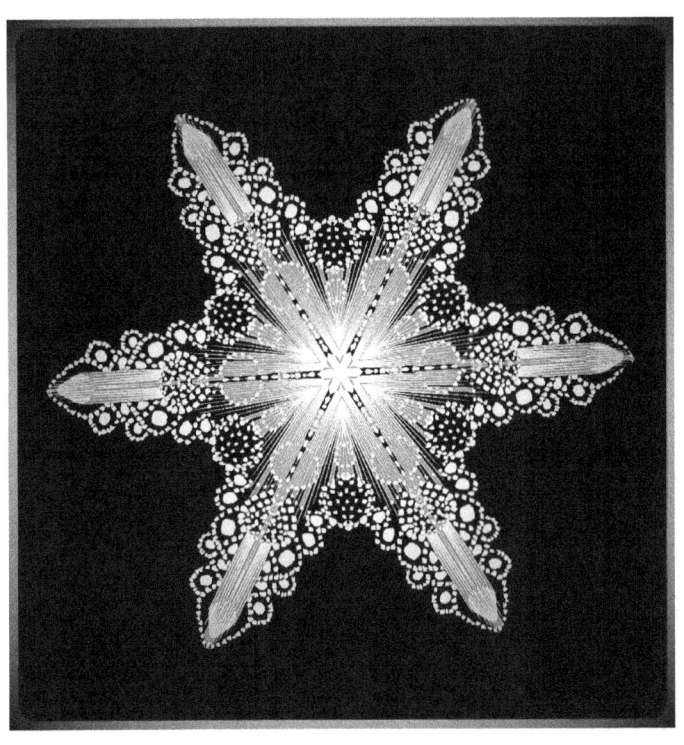

Blowing Snow

Coiling and blowing snow past weather vanes
Falling in and out of unseen air currents
And piling in corners to cover fences
Only to turn into powder and drift away
As stormy clouds sway and shed their tears

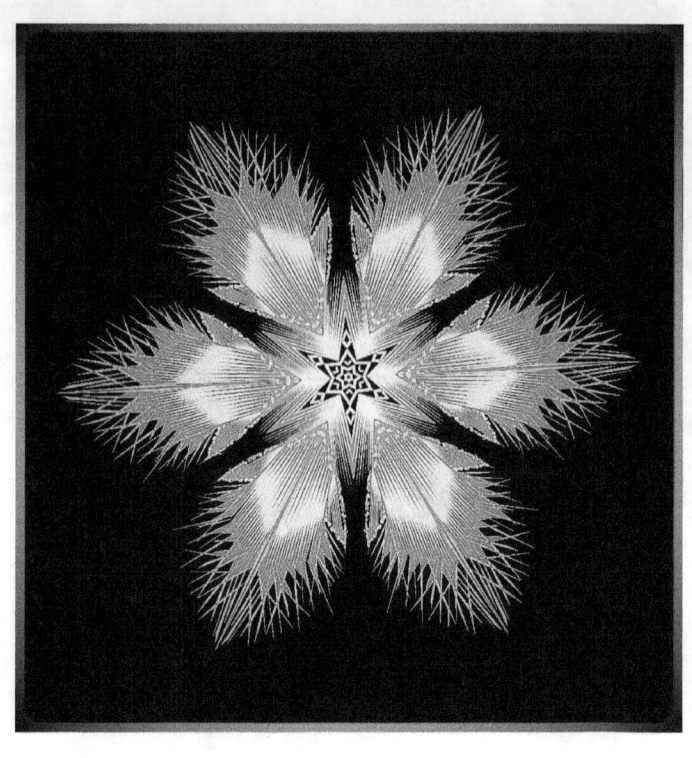

Flakes at Midnight

Black diamonds shudder and swirl
Casting a shadow on all that is clear
To show their form like floating ash
'Tis a mystery which darkens heavens
That shimmers towards glittering dawn
Becoming a snowy blanket come morn

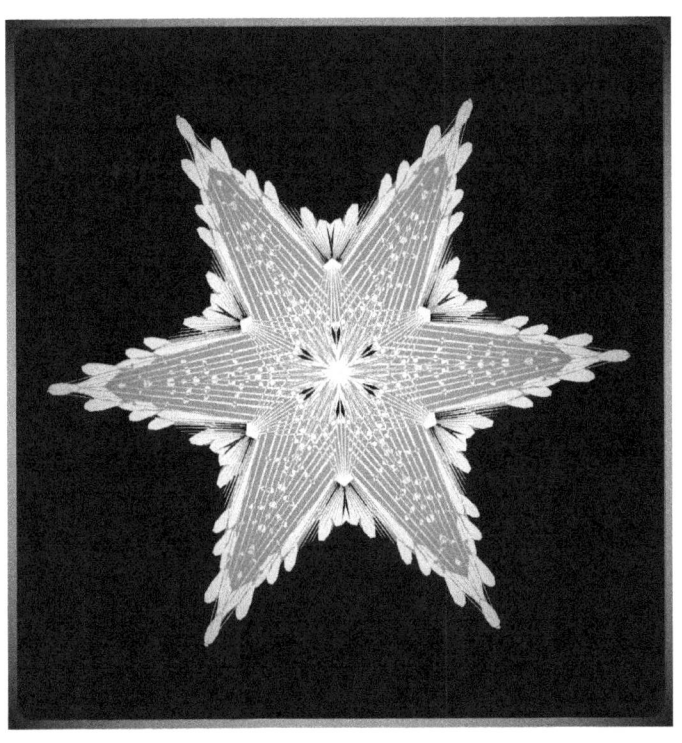

Hibernate

In down feathers on a bed of gold
With a pillow made from plush trees
And a blanket thick with ivy leaves
To lay in a cave with ice and snow
Cuddling in and out of dreamy worlds
Until Spring stirs and warm days unfold

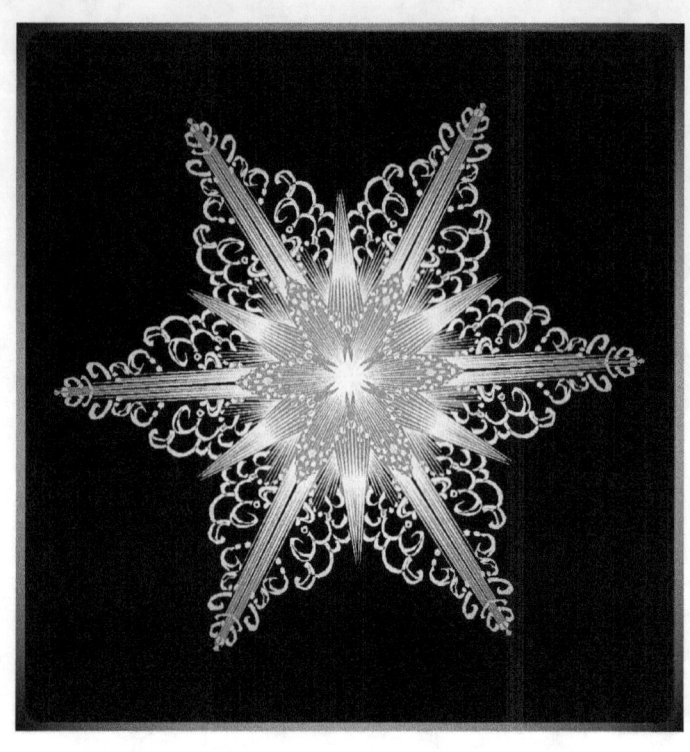

Fruitcake

Such a shamed food that tastes old
If brought out yearly- growing mold
But when it's fresh and full of love
I will eat an entire batch- truth be told

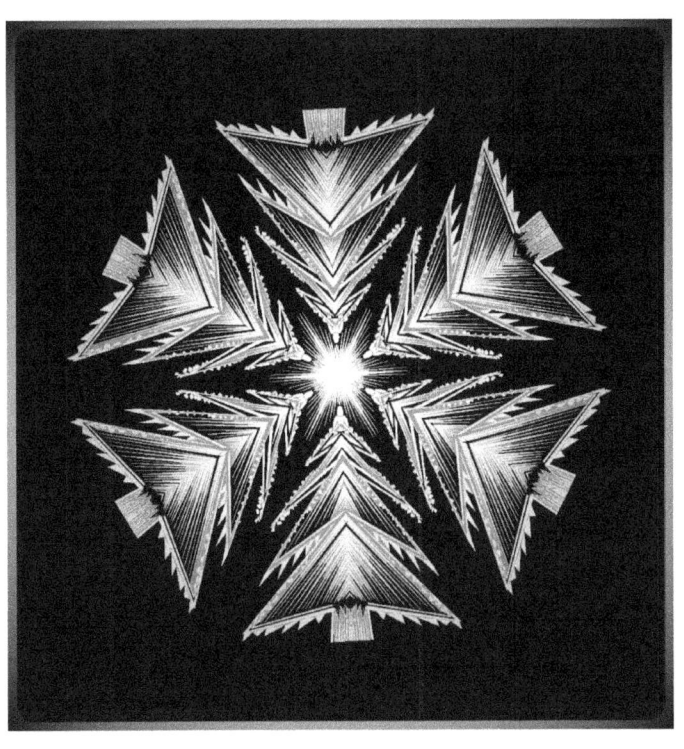

Perfect trees

If one or three; they are perfect trees
Full or barren; they speak to me
As nature decorates each one differently.
I find it impossible to cut one down
But will leave them intact indefinitely
And reuse my fake Christmas tree

APPENDIX

These are the http://snowdays.me/ flake
numbers which coincide with each photo in the
order they appear in the book.

1.	13487376
2.	13497827
3.	13528983
4.	13531571
5.	13545374
6.	13545417
7.	13546190
8.	13548187
9.	13549367
10.	13549674
11.	13552494
12.	13561488
13.	13562212
14.	13562923
15.	13563160
16.	13564067
17.	13576105
18.	13578175
19.	13578713
20.	13579112
21.	13579981
22.	13587755
23.	13594214
24.	13600047

25.	13600681
26.	13752372
27.	13752519
28.	13759522
29.	13782306
30.	13801148
31.	13808726
32.	13816390
33.	13818714
34.	13820120
35.	13853828
36.	13857454
37.	13859697
38.	13868953
39.	13870744
40.	13872610
41.	13871934
42.	13871970
43.	13872529
44.	13871687
45.	13872637
46.	13872641
47.	13872646
48.	13873747
49.	13874002
50.	13874125
51.	13618055
52.	13618479
53.	13619212
54.	13619981
55.	13622347

56.	13623907
57.	13625971
58.	13626947
59.	13629049
60.	13652961
61.	13653329
62.	13653873
63.	13660315
64.	13664028
65.	13664284
66.	13668448
67.	13683271
68.	13697680
69.	13711425
70.	13746805
71.	13748465
72.	13749550
73.	13750320
74.	13846968
75.	13850120
76.	13874334
77.	13874527
78.	13874894
79.	13875133
80.	13875702
81.	13876286
82.	13876440
83.	13876851
84.	13877438
85.	13877441
86.	13877485